Sarah Bowling's book, Road to Who[...] *people as they recover from trauma. Based on a study of the Good Samaritan parable, Sarah discloses profound revelatory insights, such as when the Good Samaritan "binds the wounds" of the victim on the Jericho Road, the word for wound in Greek is literally the word "trauma." In* Road to Wholeness, *Sarah offers understanding and wisdom to help the reader identify roots of trauma and walk a journey into recovery. Sarah co-wrote this book with her daughter, Isabell Bowling. While Sarah wrote the non-fiction part, Isabell wrote a modern allegory that helps the reader see what this timeless parable looks like in their current existence. With trauma being a major threat to the health, well-being and safety of individuals today, this book is important and very timely.*

PATRICIA KING
Author, Minister, Media Host and Producer / patriciaking.com

Trauma is a topic that is now being addressed more than ever before. Sarah Bowling, along with her daughter Isabell Bowling, brings out a refreshing revelation in Road to Wholeness. *You can experience freedom and transformation as Sarah examines the purpose of each character in the parable of the Good Samaritan. I believe this book can be the tool for overcoming whatever is holding you back from all God has for you!*

JONI LAMB
Daystar Television Network

Trauma is a lodestone of the human experience. It just seems to draw us in, even when we try to avoid it, and especially when we try to ignore it. If you are ready to work through it, Road to Wholeness *will shed light on it, not only through Sarah's sophisticated exegesis of Scripture but through her daughter Isabell's artistic rendition through fiction. Join the healing journey.*

MARK MOORE
Teaching Pastor and Author, *Core 52*

In Road to Wholeness, *Sarah and Isabell use biblical principles with modern insights to provide understanding for recovering from trauma. Beginning with the foundational question explored in Chapter One—"What's the Big Deal About Trauma?" The following chapters discuss the roles of individuals within the Good Samaritan parable, encouraging readers to reflect on their own identities and positions in the narratives of trauma. This thought-provoking and compassionate guide shows us how Jesus helps and leads us through our healing and his desire to make us whole.*

ALEX SEELEY
Co-Founder of The Belonging Co

I am pleased to be able to recommend to you Sarah and Isabell Bowling's book, Road to Wholeness. *It is extremely unfortunate that so many Christians have been told to seek healing for their traumatic experiences from secular doctors and non-Christian counseling services instead of showing them a path to wholeness through Jesus Christ. Jesus came and suffered, taking both our sin and our painful traumas on himself that we might be both healed and whole. He is the door to wholeness and a pain-free, joyful life. I am excited to think about the many people who will find the deliverance they seek from depression, anxiety and wounds of the soul as a result of reading this book. Blessings!*

JOAN HUNTER
Evangelist / TV Host of *Miracles Happen!*

Road to Wholeness *is a very helpful journey for anyone who is dealing with trauma, and that means all of us. Sarah and Isabell have taken an in-depth look at Jesus' parable of the Good Samaritan, provided helpful spiritual insights and modern applications. This book is important because I believe Jesus is the ultimate healer and road to wholeness in our lives!*

CECE WINANS
Recording Artist

The Bowlings have provided a most engaging picture of the Good Samaritan—one that I hadn't considered before. I heartily recommend it to you, especially if you want to be challenged, poked, and prodded out of your complacent, stale, religious perspective.

JEFF VOTH

Founder of Cavetime and Author of *Cavetime, Defending the Feminine Heart, A Thousand More Amens, Why Lewis?* and *Jesus is the Thesis* and *Serpent Crusher*

This amazing book, Road to Wholeness, *is a much-needed message for our world when the experience of personal trauma seems to be accelerating. Sarah and Isabell Bowling bring years of ministry and personal experience into this manifesto of hope that will show you the way to encounter the God of hope and healing and assist you in receiving the wholeness that brings restoration of the human soul that Jesus brought in proclaiming the good news of the Kingdom. There is healing and restoration from a life of trauma to the abundant life that Jesus promised! You will find that in* Road to Wholeness!

DR. MIKE HUTCHINGS

Director of Education, Global Awakening Ministries
President, God Heals PTSD Foundation / godhealsptsd.com

ROAD TO WHOLENESS

HEALING *from* TRAUMA

SARAH BOWLING

and ISABELL BOWLING

BREAKFAST
FOR SEVEN

I'd like to dedicate this book to Denny. Thank you Denny, for being steady, caring and a pure soul. I'm grateful for you more than words could express!

SARAH

For Dr. Voth: The girl in the back of the classroom has moved into the pages. Without your support, guidance and love, I would be gone. Thank you!
For Bekah: You're next :)

ISABELL

ISBN: 978-0-9819567-1-8 (print)
ISBN: 978-1-963492-02-6 (eBook)

Produced by Breakfast for Seven
breakfastforseven.com

Printed in the United States of America.

contents

introduction

The Good Samaritan is one of Jesus' most famous parables. Though it is a well-known story, the parable is rarely taught through the lens of trauma. When you hear the word trauma, what comes to mind? Does it make you think of some experiences that were painful to you? Trauma can be a physical experience, an emotional experience, an event, a relationship, grief or many other things. It shows up in many forms—not only in the initial encounter but also in our memories, reactions, etc.

Regardless of your education, family background, or age, we have all experienced trauma at some point. It creeps and seeps into our lives, affecting our outlook, relationships, priorities and choices. Thankfully, Jesus can help us transform our trauma so it isn't transferred to those we love and so it doesn't dominate or control our lives.

If you took an inventory of traumatic events in your life, what would you include on this list? When you think of this list of traumas in your life, could you group the various traumas into categories? Some ways that we could categorize trauma could

be in terms of severity, your age at the time of the experience, locations, how often it occurred, and the impact that it had on your life.

This book is organized into two parts. The first part will give you insight for healing from the trauma of your own story, as well as recognizing trauma in others and how you might love them as they navigate their own healing journeys. After each chapter, you will also find a worksheet section that will give you a moment to reflect as well as prompts to take inventory of your story and see yourself in light of the various characters in the parable of the Good Samaritan.

The second half of the book is a gripping retelling of the parable in a modern setting. The allegory will comfort and challenge you on your own journey with trauma and help others find redemption in their own lives.

Jesus is still healing broken hearts, and there is a road you can take today to move towards healing and wholeness. May you find healing in your heart, soul and mind as you walk through trauma. May the Lord give you the garment of praise for a spirit of heaviness, beauty for ashes and set you free from trauma to live in God's design for your life!

ROAD TO WHOLENESS

part one

chapter one

What's the Big Deal About Trauma?

"I'm not that sick. There are lots of people who need weekly therapy, but I'm not one of those."

This was my reply to a therapist who told me that she thought she could help me, and she offered me a standing weekly appointment. When I look back on that conversation now, I chuckle to myself thinking about how truly oblivious I was. That is part of the challenge we experience when it comes to trauma. It can leave us "half dead" and unaware, even oblivious, to the extent that it is affecting our daily existence, choices, priorities and general outlook on life.

Trauma is a problem that has accompanied human existence for a very, very long time. Indeed, there's not a human on the planet who hasn't experienced trauma. This means that regardless of your upbringing, socio-economic status, education, family background, religious beliefs, hobbies, physical condition, etc., we all have experienced trauma, full stop. And there are some things to consider about trauma that merit your reflection:

Trauma that is not transformed is transferred. If we ignore trauma and its tendrils, we usually pass it on to others. This goes with the adage, "Hurt people, hurt people."

Trauma creeps and seeps into our lives, affecting our outlook on life, relationships, priorities and choices. Sometimes we don't realize how much trauma is operating behind the scenes of our lives.

Everyone you meet and have relationship with has experienced various forms of trauma. It's not uncommon for people to live their lives with previous trauma being the integral driving force for their outlook and interactions.

Jesus is well-experienced in dealing with human trauma. He can help us to heal, recover from and transform the traumas that we've experienced.

Before we look at trauma, it will be helpful to understand what it is. According to the American Psychological Association, "Trauma is an emotional response to a terrible event like an accident, rape, or natural disaster."[1] Trauma is the result of abuse in all forms (verbal, physical, emotional, sexual, etc.), neglect, and/or abandonment. In our modern society, we probably have some awareness of PTSD, which stands for post-traumatic stress disorder. It's fairly common to connect PTSD with soldiers who return home from war, but a person can experience PTSD in lots of different ways, such as:

- Protection instincts that kick in while driving after experiencing a bad car wreck.

- Overwhelming emotional memories that are experienced when a person visits a location where he/she had a really bad experience.

- An inability to do something because of an associated negative experience in the past.

- Instinctual or automatic behaviors, emotions and responses that are triggered from similar negative events.

So why would we look at things that hurt us in the past? Why would anyone be interested in "re-living" past wounds and hurts? And maybe a really important question to ponder is this: Can we be free and healed from past wounds and injuries? It is my hope and prayer in this book to answer this question with a resounding, "YES!"

In order to explore this answer, we will look at one of the most well-known parables Jesus told: the Good Samaritan found in Luke 10. In this parable, Jesus speaks to a wide variety of issues (including social and religious quandaries) with trauma being the catalyst for the parable. This is what Jesus said in these verses:

"*A man was going down from Jerusalem to Jericho, and fell among robbers, and they stripped him and beat him, and went away leaving him half dead. And by chance a priest was going down on that road, and when he saw him, he passed by on the other side. Likewise a Levite also, when he came to the place and saw him, passed by on the other side. But a Samaritan, who was on a journey, came upon him; and when he saw him, he felt compassion, and came to him and bandaged up his wounds, pouring oil and wine on them; and he put him on his own beast, and brought him to an inn and took care of him. On the next day he took out two denarii and gave them to the innkeeper and said, 'Take care of him; and whatever more you spend, when I return I will repay you.'*" (vv. 30–35 NASB)

Jesus is well-experienced in dealing with human trauma. He can help us to heal, recover from and transform the traumas that we've experienced.

As you read this parable, it's probable that one of the standout characters to you is the Samaritan. When you hear the word *Samaritan*, what comes to your mind? Do you think about the organization founded by Franklin Graham, "Samaritan's Purse"? Do you think about some vague Bible thing, possibly one of those ancient countries around Israel? Do you think of someone who was kind to you during a difficult season in your life? Does the title Samaritan come to mind when you drive by the homeless panhandlers on street corners who are holding signs asking for help?

I've personally been the recipient of someone choosing to be a Good Samaritan. I have received random acts of kindness. I've also been a Good Samaritan at various times. For the most part, I felt pretty good about my actions. The whole idea around the parable of the Good Samaritan is that someone does something nice for someone who doesn't deserve such kindness. But I think it would be extremely helpful if we investigate this parable with purposeful reflection and attentive application. So, let's see what we can discover as we explore how this parable interfaces with trauma in our lives.

Conversation

The Good Samaritan story is one of Jesus' most famous parables. It's a timeless and universal story that has been told, retold, preached, taught, dissected, used to motivate, referenced, and integrated for millennia. Jesus told the Good Samaritan parable in answer to the question of a Jewish lawyer who was trying to justify himself. "Who is my neighbor?" Even before the lawyer asked Jesus this question, they had been discussing how the lawyer could inherit eternal life and what the Jewish law was about loving God and loving one's neighbor as oneself. The immediate context of the parable is Jesus' answer to the lawyer's attempt to justify himself. He was hoping to get himself off the hook by narrowing down the definition of what a neighbor was.

Instead, in His parable, Jesus broadened the definition of what a neighbor is. He also gave a powerful illustration for what it means to love. Furthermore, Jesus described humanity and human experiences on the journey of life. We will continue to look at this parable in great depth and reflection, being open to considering how we might fit into this parable in various ways.

To begin with, it's interesting to note that the Good Samaritan parable stems from a conversation with a Jewish lawyer and Jesus. The lawyer, who is an expert in Jewish law, is asking Jesus questions about Jewish law. If anyone would know the law being discussed, it would be the Jewish lawyer. I'm bringing this to your attention because it's possible that you might be well-versed in biblical knowledge, a gold-star achiever in Sunday School accomplishments, a highly moral and upright citizen, a rigorous devotee to righteous compliance, and a proponent for Christian values. Generally, all of these can be good things, as long as we maintain as the highest priority loving well and keeping in mind the people who are around us.

These two anchors, love and people, are the essential underpinnings to Jesus' conversation with the lawyer and the Good Samaritan parable. These same values need to frame and define our devotion to Jesus so that we don't fall into the quagmire in which the Jewish lawyer found himself—arguing with Jesus and trying to defend himself, looking for loopholes and ways to get off the hook. I would suggest that we are not our best selves when we try to justify ourselves with Jesus using religious jargon and platitudes.

Does this really happen in our modern world? Do people use religion to rationalize selfish decisions? For that matter, how can we help everyone? And are we really helping people and their core issues when we are soft and generous? What about the value of "tough love"? These are all good questions, and I would suppose that you could come up with more valid points for consideration. Let's save these questions and reflections for Worksheet One at the end of this chapter.

> These two anchors, love and people, are the essential underpinnings to Jesus' conversation with the lawyer and the Good Samaritan parable.

Circling back to Jesus' conversation with the Jewish lawyer, I'm extremely grateful that Jesus didn't blow off this lawyer, dismissing him for being distracted with his religious piety. Maybe Jesus could see past the lawyer's veneer because He wanted the lawyer to be more authentic with love and concerned about people. Perhaps Jesus would have similar conversations with some of us. I'd suggest that Jesus' conversation with the lawyer and with us is grounded in His deep and authentic love for us, so that we could experience genuine love rather than religious compliance and rigor.

Now that we've established the context that launched Jesus into this powerful story, let's jump into the parable.

Setting

Jesus gives the setting for the events of this parable, identifying a man walking from Jerusalem to Jericho. This road has been fairly well documented over the course of history by the likes of Josephus and others, including references in the Old Testament (2 Samuel 15:23–16:14; 2 Kings 25:4). About eighteen miles long, this road went through part of the Judean wilderness and had an elevation change of about 3,300 feet, a drastic decline from Jerusalem to Jericho. Historically, the Jericho Road was known to be full of bandits, robbers, dangerous characters and difficult experiences. The road was twisty and windy, with blind curves and dusty, dry ruts. Nevertheless, it was a well-known road that was traveled by many people, even though it was risky.

> **Historically, the Jericho Road was known to be full of bandits, robbers, dangerous characters and difficult experiences.**

Maybe the Jericho Road is a bit like our journey in life. This journey can have lots of unexpected twists, unsavory characters, dry seasons, rocky terrain and sometimes, life is just a slough in which we pick up our feet one step at a time so that we keep walking. Sometimes we set out on a journey, like starting a new school, taking a job, moving to a new city, or starting a new relationship. As we move along this journey, we will have some challenging seasons and experiences. I also know that we can also encounter different kinds of people on our journey in life, and some of these folks are hurtful.

Over the course of this book, it is my prayer that you will look at the journey of your life and consider the wide variety of ways that the Good Samaritan parable can be highly applicable and transformative. I'd like for you to consider joining a journey and conversation with Jesus. I'm inviting you to let Him talk with you about various experiences in your life, how you see yourself, the people around you, religious concerns, recovery, trauma, and redemption.

Will you join the Jericho journey to living as your best self? If you say yes to this question, then let's begin by exploring the various characters in the Good Samaritan parable as we try to see ourselves in each character.

The Road, the People, the Experiences

On the Jericho Road, there were a variety of interesting people. Take a few minutes to think about your journey in life as a road. Describe the journey of your life in the space below.

1. *What have been some good experiences or high points on your journey in life?*

2. *What have been some bad experiences or low points on your journey in life?*

3. *Who have been some helpful and kind people along your journey?*

4. *Who have been some ugly and hurtful people along your journey?*

chapter two

Who Are You?

"Who are you?
Who, who, who, who?
Who are you?
Who, who, who, who?
Who are you?
Who, who, who, who?
Who are you?
Who, who, who, who?"

This is the chorus to the famous pop hit from The Who in 1978. Supposedly, Pete Townshend (a British rockstar) was inspired to write this song after he met with music publishers in New York and was really discouraged from his meeting.[2]

While the lyrics to this song are simple and maybe boring because the are repetitive, I think that the identity question is one that every human on the planet asks himself or herself. Who are you?

This identity question is something each of us has wrestled with and will wrestle with in various ways and in a variety of contexts over the course of our lives. These battles show up in the peer groups that we choose and reject in our school age years. The struggles are continued when we try to choose a profession or major in college, and they continue when we enter the workforce and make changes in our jobs and relationships.

When I think about my life, I've leaned into various identities, activities and relationships in the exploration of my identity. Here are a few examples of exploring who I am not and who I am on the journey to becoming my true self:

In my elementary school, it was a big deal to get into fights and stand up for oneself. I learned that I didn't really like fighting. I'd avoid or chicken out when I was supposed to show up and defend myself. I'm a better fugitive than fighter.

In middle and high school, I wanted to be an incredible basketball player, so I sank a lot of time and energy into this pursuit. I also enjoyed the camaraderie of being on a team, working toward a common goal, winning, working hard, activity, training, developing skills and abilities along with lots of personal fulfillment. But alas, I learned from a very honest camp counselor that despite my dreams and fantasies, I wasn't going to be anything more than a kind of average and highly enthusiastic basketball player.

In college, I wanted to be really smart, so I picked physics as my first major. I thought that sounded highly intelligent. I quickly learned that this degree was overflowing with landmines and disasters for me because I didn't have the intellectual acumen for this type of learning. Instead, by accident, I discovered that I have a natural gift for languages. I quickly changed my degree to German and experienced lots more success.

After getting married, I wasn't too keen on exploring the parenting scenario for a few years. When I started having kids, I discovered a whole new piece of me that was highly fulfilled in being a mom.

I think that the identity question is one that every human on the planet asks himself or herself. Who are you?

With relationships, I've had lots of friendships that revolved around activities or various seasons in my life. These included the proverbial soccer mom and pickleball friendships (common activities), workplace relationships (common goals), along with friendships that were seasonal because of the overlapping and shared experiences. I've come to learn that relationships can often help us discover who we are as well as who we are not.

As for my relationship with God, this has been an interesting journey over the course of my life. I've explored not just different church experiences but also dug deeply into the Bible to learn about who God is as well as who God is not. It's been really powerful to become increasingly convinced that God loves me because that's who God is. As such, I'm incapable of changing God or changing Love when I'm less or more pious.

With all these observations, I'd suggest to you that we can grow in the understanding of who we are, as well as who we are not, as we look at both experiences and seasons in our lives. All of this is important when we think about the Good Samaritan parable and its involvement with trauma because we need to consider that we could be each character in this parable.

It's been really powerful to become increasingly convinced that God loves me because that's who God is.

When you think about it, this parable has six characters who play important roles. These six individuals include the traveler (victim/patient), bandits or criminals, a priest, a Levite, the hero (also known as the Good Samaritan), and the innkeeper. I'm bringing all of these characters to your attention because in this parable, we often only think about the traveler/victim and the hero/Samaritan. Of course, these are very important individuals in this parable, but we would be remiss to ignore the other participants.

Furthermore, as we think about this parable and begin to unpack it for the maximum impact and help it can have with trauma in our lives, it's important to look at what characters we might identify with most easily. Who might you be in the Good Samaritan story?

Do you see yourself as the *hero* in the parable? Do you find yourself stopping to help people, having compassion for people who are going through difficult experiences? Would you consider the Good Samaritan to be your role model?

While some of us may want to be like the hero in this parable, there are many of us who relate to the guy who got beat up in the story. Do you most easily identify with the *victim* on the Jericho Road? It's possible that some of us see ourselves as continual victims, getting ripped off or hurt by people and an unfortunate traveler on the journey of life.

In relation to the *priest and Levite* in the story, it's possible that we don't want to identify with these men because they seem heartless and cold. But maybe we have more in common with these men than on first glance. Could we be the religious priest or Levite who sees the half-dead man along the roadside as we go along the journey of life? Is it possible that we are too busy with our church responsibilities that we don't have time to stop for someone in need? Do we think that people in dire straits are probably just getting what they deserve? Do we excuse ourselves from helping someone because they're ugly, broken, smelly, repulsive, wholly other, or just too far beyond our abilities and resources?

Is it possible that you might be one of the *bandits* that traumatizes the traveler on the Jericho Road? I seriously doubt that many of us set out to hurt someone over the journey of our lives. But it's possible that we've said hurtful or even hateful things to people, injuring their souls. It's possible that we've abandoned or neglected people whom we've known to be hurt.

Are you the *innkeeper* who is an ambivalent bystander, just taking care of your property or income? Do injured people show up in your life for a season, and you help them on their road to recovery? Have you led or participated in a small group that was helpful for people recovering from trauma? In a modern context, the small group scenario could be similar to the innkeeper in the Good Samaritan parable.

Do we excuse ourselves from helping someone because they're ugly, broken, smelly, repulsive, wholly other, or just too far beyond our abilities and resources?

I'm asking you about each of these characters in this parable because there's good value in considering who we are at various times in our lives and in various contexts. Generally, I think that we usually gravitate toward identifying with either the Good Samaritan (hero) of the parable or the beat-up victim, traumatized and half dead along the roadside doing the journey of life. Maybe we gravitate toward one or the other of these characters because they are the most obvious in the story. But I think that it's both helpful and important to look at each of the characters in this parable and see how we might relate to each person. And as we think about each character, considering how we might relate to each one, we can grow and see that trauma touches all of us in a variety of ways.

In the next few chapters, we'll explore each character, learning about their historical context and what the Jewish lawyer understood about these characters when Jesus inserted them into the story. Remember that Jesus told the Good Samaritan parable as an answer to the Jewish lawyer trying to justify himself by asking, "Who is my neighbor?" As you read each chapter, you might find it helpful to review the fiction chapter associated with each character to see what that could look like in our modern existence. To further help you think about each individual in the parable, there are worksheets at the end of each chapter that you can use to explore your experiences and the possible alignments with each character.

To help you think about your identity, consider doing Worksheet Two that goes with this chapter.

Who Are You?

Knowing who you are in Christ is so important. The more you study the Bible, the more you will discover who God made you to be. Pray and then spend some time thinking through these questions.

1. *Describe your elementary years in school. Things that could be helpful to include would be: activities that you loved and loathed; friendships that were enjoyable as well as those that were not enjoyable. Describe why for each friendship.*

2. *What was your upbringing like? Did you have a stable home? Was there lots of chaos or upheaval in your home? Did you have siblings? How many? What were your parents/caregivers like? Did they pay attention to you? Were they consistent and present? Did you have support with school and/or activities?*

3. *Who are you now, and what are your top three priorities?*

4. Have you taken any personality tests like Myers-Briggs, DISC, Enneagram, Big Five, etc.? What are the results of any of these tests?

5. When you think about these results, how would your personality interface with each character in the Good Samaritan parable?

traveler:

bandit:

priest:

Levite:

hero:

innkeeper:

chapter three

Trauma and a Hero

When you think about heroes, what comes to your mind? Depending on your interests and age, you might say that various movie characters are heroes, like Captain America or Wonder Woman. You might consider that a political leader or humanitarian is a hero, or maybe you had a teacher or coach in school that could be a hero for you. It's important that we recognize that there are heroes in our modern world. Here's an example of a living hero we can look to.

Leroy Smith is a man who was caught between two realities in the state he serves. One day, the African-American state trooper donned a civilian suit to watch as South Carolina rolled up the Confederate flag flying over its state Capitol;[3] as the *New York Times* reports in a profile, sending "chills running along his spine" as a racially divisive symbol of the Confederacy was consigned to history.[4] Eight days later, he was back at the Capitol—this time in uniform—as protesters decried the flag's removal, gently guiding an older white supremacist, seemingly overcome by the heat, to a couch inside the air-conditioned State House in a photo that went almost immediately viral.[5] Smith's explanation? "I think that's the greatest thing in the world—love," he says. "And that's why so many people were moved by it."

"He looked fatigued, lethargic—weak," said Smith of the unidentified man, who was clad in a white supremacist T-shirt. "I knew there was something very wrong with him." The two men didn't talk much, notes the *Times,* other than Smith's quiet words of encouragement as they climbed the State House steps. An aide to Gov. Nikki Haley snapped the picture of the two men, unbeknownst to Smith, sensing a moment of grace as South Carolina struggled to cope with a racist tragedy.[6] "In that moment, Leroy Smith was the embodiment of all that," says Haley's aide.[7]

Considering what heroes could look like in our modern world, let's look at the hero in the Good Samaritan parable, noting his specific actions related to trauma.

"But a Samaritan, who was on a journey, came upon him; and when he saw him, he felt compassion, and came to him and bandaged up his wounds [trauma]*, pouring oil and wine on them; and he put him on his own beast, and brought him to an inn and took care of him. On the next day he took out two denarii and gave them to the innkeeper and said, 'Take care of him; and whatever more you spend, when I return I will repay you'"* (Luke 10:33–35 NASB).

When we read these verses, it is massively important that we recognize and absorb the reality that Jesus picked a very unlikely hero for this parable—the Samaritan. This hero was all the more difficult to accept for the Jewish lawyer who was hearing Jesus' story in answer to his attempt to justify himself. Remember, for Jewish people at this time, Samaritans were pretty much the scum of the earth, full stop. Indeed, Jewish prejudice against Samaritans was normal and accepted—all the more rationalized and validated with a Jewish lawyer. So Jesus' purposeful selection of a Samaritan hero was possibly appalling and repulsive to this lawyer.

Considering what heroes could look like in our modern world, let's look at the hero in the Good Samaritan parable, noting his specific actions related to trauma.

In thinking about this, I wonder who Jesus would pick in our modern world that might be unlikely or even repulsive to us. Reflecting on this idea, I'm reminded of an experience that I had when I was a teenager traveling overseas.

"This country will never amount to anything if they can't figure out how to put ice in a Coke!" This is what my dad exclaimed in a developing country when he was super frustrated about getting a warm can of Coke on a hot day. I remember sitting across the table from him when he had this meltdown, and I hoped that no one around him understood English or his outburst. I'm sure that his high-level emotional anger was clear to everyone around us, regardless of the English gap.

My parents and I were exploring a new country, and it was clear to me from the outset that my dad didn't like this country, didn't respect the people, and didn't appreciate the culture, its history or its diversity. This trip was about two weeks long, and we visited some key cities during our time. I noted at various times that different local individuals helped my dad with his luggage and with some practical things, they extended patience with his food struggles, and they tried to accommodate his preferences that were more aligned with American culture. Lots of people were gracious with my dad during this trip, but he never really enjoyed this country nor learned to enjoy the people or cultural diversity.

I'm telling you about this experience because we can all have struggles with people who are different than us. We can all have challenges engaging with and being respectful toward others who are not like us, with whom we disagree or struggle to find common ground. It's possible that you might think of these individuals as "other" to yourself or maybe even find them distasteful or repulsive: homeless, different ethnicity, obese, homosexual, unchurched, elderly/retired, Muslim, fitness fiends, wealthy, uneducated, tattooed, youth/teenagers, extroverts, etc. No doubt that there are plenty of options for us to see people as "other" or different from ourselves.

Over the course of history, America has had very significant struggles with navigating ethnic diversity and prejudice. I haven't really struggled with ethnic diversity, but I've had more than a few internal challenges in navigating economic disparity, educational gaps, fashion and beauty priorities, etc. I've had more than a few times in my life when I looked down on someone because they weren't educated, didn't have social etiquette, struggled with athletic coordination, didn't align with my religious values, didn't speak English, etc. And there have been innumerable times when I felt "less than" because of my struggles to be fashionable or to be comfortable around very accomplished or affluent people.

No doubt that there are plenty of options for us to see people as "other" or different from ourselves.

It's important for us to look at prejudices that we may have because this was exactly what Jesus did in the Good Samaritan parable. As you read through this chapter, keep this question in the back of your mind: Who are people that are difficult for me?

It's noteworthy that Jesus chose a Samaritan to be the hero in this story. This stands out because Jesus is speaking directly to a Jewish lawyer in answering his question about who his neighbor was. It's shocking that Jesus chose a Samaritan as the hero because at this time in history, most Jews hated Samaritans. At a minimum, they saw this group of people as inferior and half-breeds to God's chosen people, the Jews. It wasn't uncommon for Jews to altogether avoid Samaritans, talk about them with disdain and be thoroughly repulsed by any contact with them.

The fact that Jesus chose a Samaritan to be the hero in this parable is almost a hostile assault on the lawyer's revulsion for Samaritans. Let's consider some interesting things about Samaritans so that we can better understand this hero.

Samaritans generally lived in Samaria, which was the area between Galilee on the north and Judea to the south. The people who lived in this area were considered to be the "left-overs" from when Babylon invaded the Northern Kingdom of Israel and took thousands of Jews to Babylon as exiles. The Samaritans adhered to the Pentateuch (the first five books of the Old Testament) and the main place for their worship was on Mount Gerizim rather than the temple in Jerusalem where the Jews centered their worship. Samaritans didn't appreciate being dismissed and derided by Jews, so there was no love lost between these two groups of people.

It's important for us to look at prejudices that we may have because this was exactly what Jesus did in the Good Samaritan parable.

When we think about the dynamics between Jews and Samaritans, it's all the more powerful to reflect on the choices and actions of the Good Samaritan, particularly when we remember that the Jericho Road is squarely situated in Jewish territory and somewhat remote from Samaria. It could be customary or expected to be kind and compassionate to one's own countryman. Indeed, hospitality in the Middle East is a significant and pervasive cultural value, even to this day. However, it's a whole different thing to be kind and compassionate in "enemy" territory and it's even more astounding that an "enemy" was over-the-top compassionate to someone who could be hostile and derogatory if they weren't impaired and brutalized.

Furthermore, it's very powerful to understand that when the Samaritan bound the wounds of the victim on the Jericho Road, the word for *wound* in Greek is literally our word "trauma." So in this parable, Jesus is addressing several important themes, and trauma is the central catalyst around which the observers reacted. To this end, maybe it would be helpful for us to remember that everyone we encounter in our lives has experienced some form of trauma.

In addition to our awareness of trauma, it's vitally important that we consider the incredible choices and actions the Samaritan took to heal the brutalized victim. The Good Samaritan saw the beat-up man, had compassion on him and came to him. He bandaged the man's wounds, pouring into them oil and wine (antiseptic and a soothing salve). He lifted the victim onto his beast of burden and led him to an inn where he took care of him. The next day, the Samaritan gave the innkeeper some money to look after the beat-up guy and let the innkeeper know that he would return and pay off any debts that the victim might incur for his recovery.

The extreme efforts that the Samaritan took to ensure the recovery of the traumatized man are truly astounding when we pause to consider the enormity of everything that he did. In latter sections of this book, we will look in depth at the actions/verbs that the Good Samaritan did and what such actions look like as they relate to trauma.

In the meantime, as I write this chapter, I find myself reflecting on various people who have helped me in traumatic experiences over the course of my life. In one experience, I was in my early twenties and was studying in a very small and remote town in Germany. At university, German was my major, so I was there for the summer to attend a language school and earn some college credits. As I planned for this experience in the spring semester, I was super excited to get to have this adventure.

The extreme efforts that the Samaritan took to ensure the recovery of the traumatized man are truly astounding when we pause to consider the enormity of everything that he did.

When I landed at the home of my host family, I was less than excited. The mom was rattling on in German (which I didn't understand well) and showing me how to feed her cat, do the dishes, run the dishwasher and what cupboards were "verboten." I didn't understand about eighty percent of what she said. After a day or so, she was never around. I found myself living with two men, an older gentlemen and a younger guy whom I suppose was the son of the hostess. I wasn't too keen on this living arrangement.

Additionally, the house to which I was assigned was a fair distance away from the language institute, so it was a long trek to get to class and home every day. I quickly began to feel isolated and lonely, except for Gustavo and Maria Sivio. This was a young couple from Argentina, and Gustavo was also attending the same language institute. We were in the same class. This couple took me under their wing during the whole summer and gave me friendship and a boatload of laughing, such that I had their relationship to help me stay sunny and distanced from depression and loneliness. They were an unlikely and unexpected friendship to me, for which I'm massively grateful to this day.

Who Is Your Enemy?

When we consider that the Samaritan was the least likely person to go to such extravagant extremes to help the severely trauma-tized Jewish man, it's necessary for us to look into our own lives and perspectives to identify some "least likely" suspects.

1. *For starters, who would be some groups of people that have been, or who are currently, difficult for you? Circle the groups of people that have been/are challenging for you.*

poor	*educated*	*homeless*
wealthy	*uneducated*	*athletes*
Caucasians	*African Americans*	*Hispanics*
Asians	*fashionistas*	*manual laborers*
immigrants	*LGBTQ+*	*bohemians*
atheists	*churchies*	*conservatives*
introverts	*extroverts*	*liberals*
heathens	*Bible thumpers*	*addicts*

2. *In this space, list additional pockets or groups of people with whom you have or do struggle.*

3. *Describe an experience when you had some negative interaction with one or more of these groups.*

4. *Do you have any current interactions with individuals from one or more of these groups? What does that look like?*

5. Describe how you would feel if Jesus made someone a hero from one of these groups that is challenging for you.

6. Have you ever been a hero to or helped someone who is drastically different from you? What was that like, and how did you feel in that experience?

chapter four

The Victim/Patient

*"'Love the Lord your God with all your heart and with
all your soul and with all your strength and with all
your mind'; and, 'Love your neighbor as yourself.'"*

LUKE 10:27

"You're so ugly, you can't play with us!"

"Ick! Your face is disgusting!"

"Run away so you don't catch her disease!"

These were some of the things I heard when I showed up to
school in first grade after I tripped on the asphalt paving at recess
and ripped chunks of skin off my face. When this happened, the
recess monitor shuffled me off to the school nurse where she
cleaned off the grit and gravel that was enmeshed with the skin

and blood all over my face. They sent me home for the afternoon because I was pretty shaken up.

I was supposed to not wear any Band-Aids for a day or so to give the wounds time to breathe, so when I turned up at school the next morning, many of my classmates ran away from me. Of course, that really hurt my feelings, so I was doubly injured.

I share this experience because all of us experience trauma that could include things like:

- Scraping your face across asphalt in elementary.

- Getting berated by a teacher for being "stupid."

- Being molested in childhood.

- Suffering the loss of a parent, spouse, child, or friend.

- Being ostracized in middle or high school.

- Getting fired from a job in a very hurtful way.

- Being in a horrible car wreck.

- Experiencing combat overseas or seeing a horrible shooting.

- Going through a really hurtful breakup or divorce.

These are a few examples of trauma that you might have experienced. The truth of the matter is that being human means that we will experience trauma. While none of us like this truth, it is nonetheless our human reality. Thankfully, Jesus acknowledged that truth in His Good Samaritan parable. Consider the beginning of this story in Luke 10:30. *"A man was going down from Jerusalem to Jericho, and fell among robbers, and they stripped him and beat him, and went away leaving him half dead"* (NASB).

Sometimes, we go through life and unexpected bad things happen to us, like the victim in the Good Samaritan parable. In Jesus' story, the victim is walking along the road from Jerusalem to Jericho. This road was very well known and used for commerce, transporting military groups and visiting Jerusalem for worship purposes since the Jewish temple was there.

The Jericho Road was well known because of how much it was used. It was also well-known because it was filled with shady characters who hid in caves and around blind curves to attack people walking on this road, victimizing them for sport or pleasure and stealing whatever they could. Furthermore, the road was eighteen miles long and almost entirely devoid of vegetation, water supplies and human contact. Walking on this road would be like walking in Death Valley in Eastern California—desolate, hot, rocky and barren.

Coming back to our parable, the guy is walking away from Jerusalem and toward Jericho when a pack of these shady characters jump him. The first thing they do is strip the traveler of his clothes. If we pause to think about that, being attacked and stripped naked is an extremely traumatic experience. The exposure, embarrassment, humiliation and helplessness would be bad just for that experience alone. It's also possible that sexual abuse would be associated with a person being stripped naked.

Furthermore, the bandits pressed the experience by beating their victim. In the Greek, it says that "they laid plagues" on the man. This beating was so severe that the victim was half-dead when they finished their violence and aggression. He was so brutally beaten that half of his life was gone—beaten out of him. When they finished with their savagery, they left their victim along the roadside.

> **Sometimes, we go through life and unexpected bad things happen to us, like the victim in the Good Samaritan parable.**

All of these actions are important because each of the three activities resulted in trauma that was observed by individuals who were also walking along the Jericho Road. As for the victim, the first traumatic experience was having his clothes stolen and being left naked. The second traumatic experience was when he was beaten and mauled by the bandits. Finally, when the barbarians abandoned and left the man on the roadside half dead, that was also traumatic.

In the simplest descriptions, trauma is the result that happens from at least one, if not all three, injuries or experiences. Trauma can be the result of exposure (nakedness), abuse (physical, emotional or mental), and neglect. Trauma happens when a person experiences one, two or all three of these pains. In this parable, Jesus describes what happens when someone undergoes trauma. Jesus uses the Greek word for trauma when He begins to describe the activities of the Good Samaritan. He said that the Good Samaritan binds the victim's wounds. As a reminder, the word *wound* in Greek is the word for *trauma*. So the victim on the Jericho Road suffered from three kinds of trauma: exposure, abuse and neglect.

The problem with trauma is that it is an echo of past pain that can influence and even control the present. Probably the most familiar and modern concept of trauma that you might be aware of is the term PTSD, which stands for Post-Traumatic Stress Disorder. In the simplest terms, PTSD refers to the mental and emotional ripples that can occur after a person experiences a traumatic event. It is frequently associated with soldiers who return from war and have ongoing mental and emotional health struggles from what they observed and experienced during their deployment.

This is an example from Osvaldo Gutierrez, a Marine Corps veteran returning to his home and struggling with PTSD.

"I served in the Marine Corps in Iraq at the beginning of the invasion. Because we were there so early in the mission, we didn't know what was going to happen or what to expect. I witnessed a lot of death, both on the enemy's side and on our own. I watched friends lose their lives, and it took time for me to digest everything that I went through in that short amount of time. The transition out of the Marines was difficult, as I went from a highly stressful situation to being at home, where everyone was just living a normal life. I had nightmares and anxiety attacks when I came home and started drinking heavily to cope. For a time, I was homeless, just trying to make it from day to day. At first, I refused to reach out for help because I was just going to man up and deal with it. But when I met the woman who is now my wife, things changed. She gave me the courage to talk about what was going on in my mind. I told her everything, and though she didn't understand the experiences, she was the support system I needed to seek help. I'm now a husband and father, working to be healthy for my family. And I get to help other veterans who are in the same place I was. I tell them to find the solution that works for them—therapy, getting closer to family, whatever it is. You can succeed and overcome anything."[8]

While PTSD is most commonly associated with war veterans, we need to appreciate that people who haven't participated in the military can also experience PTSD. Consider this story from Kinoko, who is from Japan.[9]

"I was diagnosed with PTSD after experiencing the horrors of the Tōhoku earthquake and tsunami on March 11, 2011.[10] I was at home when I experienced the earthquake. Since then, I have had nightmares of dying in an earthquake at least once a week. As a result, I suffer from sleep disorders. Hearing an earthquake alert or a similar sound can cause tears or panic attacks. I got sick both physically and mentally. I suffer from depression, anxiety disorders, adjustment disorders, and autonomic imbalances. Every March 11, Japanese TV and the internet are filled with news and special reports to commemorate the victims of the disaster. Although it's important to remember the tragedy, it's important for people suffering from trauma to escape from scary and unpleasant things, and protect themselves. So, I spend this day ignoring the TV and the internet."

I think it can be helpful to hear about other people's experiences with trauma in a modern context so that the victim in the Good Samaritan parable doesn't seem so distant or foreign to us. This is important for us not only to be aware of the experiences that others have but also to think about our own experiences and possibilities with trauma. Remember, trauma can be the result of:

- Exposure
- Abuse
- Neglect

Within the context of considering the various ways these three experiences can invoke trauma in your life, let's take a brief pause to think about Jesus and His encounters with pain and suffering. You could probably see Jesus stepping in to heal victims who were suffering from trauma. You might recall His redemptive words to the woman who was caught in adultery, exposed, humiliated and on the cusp of being stoned to death by religious leaders invoking legalistic piety (John 8:1–11). When Jesus sent away her accusers, He said to her, *"I do not condemn you, either. Go. From now on sin no more"* (v. 11 NASB).

Additionally, He told the woman who was healed from her issue of blood after twelve years of pain with no help from doctors, *"Daughter, your faith has made you well; go in peace"* (Luke 8:48 NASB). It's clear that Jesus healed people who suffered from the effects and debilitations of trauma. But I'd like for you to consider that Jesus, Himself, also experienced the three inputs that lead to trauma.

Exposure: For starters, Jesus suffered from exposure (Matthew 27:28–35). Most historians and theologians agree that Jesus was crucified and hung on the cross naked, which the Romans did to humiliate their victims.

Abuse: Additionally, we know that Jesus was brutally beaten and scourged before He was forced to carry His cross to Golgotha. *"Pilate then took Jesus and scourged Him"* (John 19:1 NASB). Scourging was an extremely horrific and brutal punishment the Romans used. Here's a description of Roman scourging using a "flagellum," the instrument for scourging:

"A Roman implement for severe bodily punishment. Horace calls it horrible flagellum. It consisted of a handle, to which several cords or leather thongs were affixed, which were weighted with jagged pieces of bone or metal, to make the blow more painful and effective. It is comparable, in its horrid effects, only with the Russian knout. The victim was tied to a post and the blows were applied to the back and loins, sometimes even, in the wanton cruelty of the executioner, to the face and the bowels. In the tense position of the body, the effect can easily be imagined. So hideous was the punishment that the victim usually fainted and not rarely died under it."[11]

Neglect: Finally, Jesus knew and felt what it was like to be neglected and abandoned. Consider what He said as He hung on the cross just before He died. *"My God, My God, why have You forsaken Me?"* (Matthew 27:46 NASB). Hanging on the cross, naked and horrifically beaten, Jesus experienced abandonment, which is a third input to trauma.

To be sure, Jesus was well acquainted with trauma and even died in the throes of experiencing trauma. Jesus is aware of what it means to be human and go through exposure, abuse and neglect. Jesus knows trauma. Consider these verses that speak about Jesus being familiar with our human existence:

He was despised and forsaken of men, a man of sorrows and acquainted with grief; and like one from whom men hide their face He was despised, and we did not esteem Him. Surely our griefs He Himself bore, and our sorrows He carried; yet we ourselves esteemed Him stricken, smitten of God, and afflicted. But He was pierced through for our transgressions, He was crushed for our iniquities; the chastening for our well-being fell upon Him, and by His scourging we are healed. All of us like sheep have gone astray, each of us has turned to his own way; but the LORD has caused the iniquity of us all to fall on Him. He was oppressed and He was afflicted, yet He did not open His mouth; like a lamb that is led to slaughter, and like a sheep that is silent before its shearers, so He did not open His mouth (Isaiah 53:3–7 NASB).

With this in mind, every human has experienced and suffered from trauma. Take some time to do Worksheet Four to help you identify some of the traumas that have happened to you.

Trauma Assessment

If you're human, then you've experienced trauma, full stop. Some of the trauma that we have experienced has been situational, like when I was about eight years old. We were on a flight to Israel and had just left JFK airport. The pilot had turned off the seat-belt sign and everyone was getting situated and comfortable for the long flight. Suddenly, there was a really big boom and the plane lost altitude. After some moments, there was a mechanical sound under the plane and the noise of gushing fluid followed by the same mechanical sound. Everyone was rattled and curious about these unexpected noises.

Then the pilot came on the plane's PA system and explained that the first sound was our right engine suddenly stopping functioning. The second sound was the fuel release doors opening at the bottom of the plane, and the gushing liquid was the pilot releasing most of the plane's fuel so that we could safely return to the airport. When we landed, the runway was strewn with emergency vehicles, the likes of numerous firetrucks, ambulances, etc. This was a traumatic experience.

1. *Think of a situation in your life that was traumatic and describe it in the space below. In addition to your description, express your feelings and any subsequent ripples or aftershocks that are associated with that event.*

2. *Think of a time in your life when you experienced violence or aggression toward you. This can be physical and/or verbal. Describe that experience in the space below, along with your feelings and aftereffects.*

3. *Think of a time in your life when you experienced neglect or abandonment. This can also be rejection or intentional exclusion. Describe that experience in the space below, along with your feelings and the aftermath.*

chapter five

The Bad Dude Bandits

In reply Jesus said: "A man was going down from Jerusalem to Jericho, when he was attacked by robbers. They stripped him of his clothes, beat him and went away, leaving him half dead."

LUKE 10:30

Why would someone intentionally hurt someone else? This is an interesting question to think about because I suspect that many of us don't purposefully set out to hurt another person. So why do humans experience hurt from others?

In the last chapter, I talked about how I fell at recess in first grade and scraped my face badly. What I didn't mention in that story is that one of my classmates tripped me, causing me to fall and scrape up my face. So why would my classmate trip me? Was it an accident? Did he do it on purpose?

I've thought about these questions, and I'll never know what was in the thoughts or intents of my classmate. I can, however, say that he was from a really broken home; he showed up to school routinely smelling like urine; he didn't have clean clothing; and he knew things in first grade that were foreign and baffling to me. When I talked with my parents about him, they wisely responded that he probably came from a very difficult home life—perhaps unstable with inconsistent money, food and adequate care.

I'm making you aware of these things because there's an axiom that's important to process and digest: hurt people, hurt people. I would suggest that my friend who tripped me at recess in first grade was reacting from the hurt and neglect he was experiencing in his home life. And it's also possible that you and I have hurt people in our lives in response to the pain that we have in our own souls. Hurt people, hurt people.

It's also very true that some people are just downright mean, hurtful and hateful. Some people experience great pleasure from inflicting pain on others, and that's something that I'm not keen to explore nor understand.

Nevertheless, as we think about the reality of people hurting each other, let's consider the characters in the Good Samaritan parable who afflicted the pain on the Jericho Road traveler. In Luke we read, *"A man was going down from Jerusalem to Jericho, and fell among **robbers**, and they stripped him and beat him, and went away leaving him half dead"* (NASB).

In another translation it says, *"A Jewish man was traveling from Jerusalem down to Jericho, and he was attacked by **bandits**. They stripped him of his clothes, beat him up, and left him half dead beside the road"* (NLT).

People who do bad things could be considered bandits. There are bad folk, and we want to keep our distance from them. Such folk could include famous people like these outlaws: Osama bin Laden, Charles Manson, Harvey Weinstein, Al Capone, Julian Assange, and others. But it's fairly unlikely that we will have interactions with the likes of these kinds of outlaws. Nevertheless, we do interact with yucky people fairly often, and it's also possible that we can be a yucky person from time to time.

And it's also possible that you and I have hurt people in our lives in response to the pain that we have in our own souls. Hurt people, hurt people.

I'd suggest that we all encounter unpleasant, ugly, hateful and violent people. And if we're honest, sometimes we can possibly be one or more of these adjectives. In relation to the bandits in the Good Samaritan parable, who were these people? It's interesting to consider these individuals because most Bible translations identify the villains in the Good Samaritan story as robbers. But that's not what Jesus said.

If they were just robbers, the Greek word that would have been used would be something similar to our word *kleptomaniac*, because *klepto* is the Greek word for stealing. In this passage, however, Jesus uses the Greek word *lestais,* which is a significantly different word than robber or kleptomaniac. In the Greek, *lestais* includes thievery in its definition but drastically expands it to integrate violence, physical aggression and brutality. As a result, I prefer to use the word "bandit" rather than "robber" because of the violence and aggression that go well beyond just thievery. In our modern vernacular, we could call such a person a monster, bully or barbarian.

In Jesus' story, these were really bad guys. They jumped and stripped their victim as he walked along the road. Why would these renegades steal their victim's clothing? It's an interesting question to consider. For that matter, why does anyone take someone else's clothing to leave them exposed and entirely naked? The argument could be made that a person steals another person's clothing because they want the attire. This is certainly plausible on the desolate Jericho Road. It's also possible that stealing the victim's clothing was the opportunity to not only shame and humiliate but also sexually abuse their victim. The nakedness and exposure could have been the precursors to more exploitive actions.

I think this is a real possibility because the next action that happens in the parable is the bandits "laying plagues," literally beating their victim. Jesus doesn't give any description beyond the two words, laying plagues. I suspect that He knew that His listeners would understand the combination of these words. In our modern world, we also have enough awareness to understand what it means to get beat up.

When I was growing up, the elementary school I attended was fairly rough—I went to a school within the Denver public school district. This was during the peak of the bussing initiative, which was a national push to integrate public schools. Everyone who attended my elementary school came from an extremely diverse array of communities, ethnicities, financial abilities, educational backgrounds, and social situations. My school was very much a melting pot and a blend of very diverse students. At the same time, it was a really big deal to get into fights. I saw more than a few students get beat up at recess, head to the nurse's office and get first aid for their injuries. Getting beat up wasn't something attractive to me, nor was I on the side of beating up someone else.

In our modern world, we also have enough awareness to understand what it means to get beat up.

Consequently, when I read about the traveler on the Jericho Road getting beat up, it brings back memories of seeing bloody and beaten kids in my school. Such violence is disturbing to me, even more than forty years later. It's also challenging for me to understand how a person moves into such a highly aggressive mode that they choose to inflict pain on someone. However, the final act that these bandits did in this parable—abandoning—isn't as difficult for me to understand because of many experiences in my childhood.

I remember going on a snowmobile ride in Minnesota when I was about five years old. It was late in the afternoon, and dusk was setting in as I rode on the back of the snowmobile being driven by the eighteen-year-old daughter of my mom's friend. As we were tooling along, the engine sputtered. I hopped off the snowmobile so the driver could check the engine and get the snowmobile back to zooming along.

The driver quickly fixed whatever wasn't working and drove away before I could get back on the snowmobile. As she drove away, I remember the twilight sky and thinking about what I should do. I didn't know which way to walk because I hadn't paid attention to our journey. Nor did I have any ideas about what I should do because the place was very remote and there were no houses or structures I could see where someone might be able to help me. I remember feeling anxious and scared. It was cold, snowy and getting darker by the minute. Thankfully, after some time, the driver returned and apologized for leaving me stranded. She explained that she thought I got on the snowmobile after she fixed whatever was wrong. That's why she drove off. She seemed relieved to find me. I hopped on the snowmobile and we headed back to her house. Nevertheless, this experience rattled me, and I can appreciate what it feels like to be abandoned.

In thinking about the final action of these bandits, leaving or abandoning their victim alongside the road half dead, this action also inflicted trauma on the victim. Such abandonment is equally as cruel and traumatic as being beaten up. These bandits left him lifeless and devoid of help or a smidgen of hope.

In terms of the actions that the bandits took, it's possible they did these acts for a variety of reasons. Why does someone attack and lash out at another person? Why does a person abandon someone who is in desperate need? Sometimes we make these choices because we don't see that our actions are so truly harmful. Some people choose these actions because there's a twisted glee in their souls when they see another person harmed. I'd also suggest that people can choose the fight or flight action because of past trauma they've experienced. In the worksheet for this chapter, we'll look at some possible traumas in your life and how that meshes with your personality to reflect on the fight or flight response you may use in various situations.

Finally, to the people who listened to Jesus' parable, the actions of these bandits were not surprising. It was a fairly common experience to get accosted on the Jericho Road. Because this road was so dangerous and everyone knew it to be so, it's possible that the people listening to Jesus' parable considered the bandits to be a normal experience.

As we finish considering the villains in this parable, maybe it's good to recognize that as we go through our journey in life, we will meet and experience people who are less than pleasant and even harmful. Let's also pause to consider the possibility that maybe we have been an unpleasant and even harmful person to others. Maybe we have abandoned someone, said or did hurtful things to another person, or were clueless as to how our words and actions injured others, causing pain and trauma. The worksheet that goes with this chapter could be helpful to you with hurtful and possibly hurting people.

Looking at Banditry

Let's take some time to think about the whole idea of harming another person as we work in this chapter around the bandits in the Good Samaritan parable. Answer the questions below.

1. *Why would someone willingly choose to hurt another person?*

2. *When have you hurt someone (physically, verbally or emotionally), and why did you do that?*

3. Which response to trauma is your first instinct, to fight or flee?

4. How has your instinct to fight hurt someone?

5. How has your instinct to flee (abandon) hurt someone?

6. In what ways, situations or exchanges with people have you
    been like the bandits on the Jericho Road?

chapter six

Piety Gone Awry

*"A priest happened to be going down the same road, and
when he saw the man, he passed by on the other side."*

LUKE 10:31

I grew up as a pastor's kid, so I have an insider view on pastors.
I've been around lots of great pastors, and I've had my share of
not-so-whippy pastors. I was brought up with the perspective
that pastors are like shepherds, so a shepherd needs to smell
like their sheep. This means that pastors are about people, so
it's important for them to love people, be concerned for, and be
attentive to their flock (the people in their church).

With this perspective, I have been told that my dad was
the quintessential pastor, such that people say that he was very

loving and would talk with anyone and everyone. He had compassion for people, no matter what they looked like, who they were, or what they did or didn't do. His compassion for people wasn't based on a person's story or background; therefore, it was my assumption that pastors were pastoral and welcomed people with celebration and affirmation.

Imagine my shock when I experienced pastors who weren't pastoral. *How can a pastor be so hostile, cranky, judgmental and condemning?* I asked myself this question many times when I would come across a pastor who was prickly. And there have been many such folk. After some reflection, I've concluded that some people who get into the pastoring profession maybe didn't find their niche and should consider something that's more suited for their design.

Even though I was raised with the belief that pastors are all about people, I'm aware that the title "pastor" is used across a wide array of applications. I've met people who are youth pastors, teaching pastors, administrative pastors, children's pastors, etc. Sometimes these individuals are tasked with a specific age group or a specific function, like administrative support or preaching good sermons. It's interesting, therefore, to think that pastors may be focused on people or around function. But the original intent from the Bible was for pastors to be focused on proper worship and the spiritual growth of people.

I bring this to your attention because the title of pastor may be more common for us than the title of priest, which Jesus uses in the Good Samaritan parable. But both titles are grounded in facilitating worship and spiritual growth for people. To this end, pastors and priests need to give attention to people and care about them. As for priests in biblical times, they also had interactions with people, and they were responsible to facilitate proper worship and spiritual instruction.

All of this is to lay the groundwork for the first spectator in Jesus' Good Samaritan parable—the priest. Remember that in this story, a man is walking along the road from Jerusalem to Jericho, and he's brutally beaten and left half dead alongside the road. Having given that introduction, Jesus brings a spectator into the story: *"And by chance a priest was going down on that road, and when he saw him, he passed by on the other side"* (Luke 10:31 NASB).

Imagine my shock when I experienced pastors who weren't pastoral. *How can a pastor be so hostile, cranky, judgmental and condemning?*

Who was the priest in this parable? And what were Jewish priests about during Jesus' life? What were their priorities, functions, regular activities and outlooks on life? Along with these questions, why would a priest see a man brutally beaten and choose not to do anything?

To understand the priest in this parable, it will be helpful to have some exposure to the historical context for this group of people. During Jesus' time, priests were the key leaders in the Jewish religion to maintain the worship activities for Jews at the temple in Jerusalem (the proverbial headquarters) and throughout the nation of Israel. Priests were identified and given their responsibilities more than 1500 years before Jesus, when Moses came down from Mount Sinai in Exodus. In Moses' instructions derived from the time he spent with God, he articulated how to worship God—along with very detailed descriptions and requirements found throughout Exodus to Deuteronomy in the Old Testament.

The responsibilities that priests maintained included serving in the temple in Jerusalem by helping with sacrifices, doing ceremonial cleansing, facilitating worship with incense, a golden lamp stand, and the bread of presence, along with other temple activities. Priests also served in synagogues throughout the villages, towns and cities in Israel. Their services in the synagogues included reading and teaching from the Torah (the first five books in the Old Testament) along with other books in the Old Testament.

Priests were generally revered and respected throughout Israel, and they had a very powerful influence and profound impact on the daily life of a Jewish person. Priests were guardians of the Jewish faith, and they were keenly intent on keeping the nation of Israel congruent with God's laws that were outlined and detailed throughout the Old Testament. These men were very pious and saw themselves as the standard bearers for Israel to maintain a righteous relationship with God.

So, a priest walking along the Jericho Road would either be returning home to Jericho after his temple service in Jerusalem or making his way to Jerusalem for his priestly service. Upon seeing the victim alongside the road on which he was traveling, the priest keeps walking. He doesn't stop to observe, but rather goes to the far side of the road to maximize his distance from the bloody husk of the brutalized man.

Why would the priest make the decision to overtly avoid any contact with the victim on his journey? There's been plenty of speculation as to the reason(s) the priest chose to keep walking rather than stop to help this victim. It's possible that the priest chose to avoid the bloody man so that he wouldn't make himself "unclean" by touching such a battered body. According to Mosaic law, a priest would defile themselves by touching a dead body and thereby exclude himself from priestly service (Leviticus 21:1–17). This could be a simple answer to the priest's motive to avoid the broken man. If this is true, then the priest chose piety over compassion. He chose religious rigor over tender mercy. He preferred his religious position rather than human affinity with a broken man.

Along with these questions, why would a priest see a man brutally beaten and choose not to do anything?

Why else would the priest choose to walk away from the bloody victim? Maybe the priest was repelled by all the blood and gore. Maybe the priest thought it was too late to help the man who was half dead, supposing that the lifeless body was already dead. Perhaps the priest thought that if he stopped to help the victim, the attackers would pounce on him. Maybe the priest thought there wasn't anything he could do—he didn't know how to help the man and didn't have anything with him to provide first aid.

As we think about these possible reasons, we also have to keep in mind that this is a parable that Jesus is telling to the Jewish lawyer in answer to his question about who is his neighbor. The parable is fiction—it didn't actually happen, although it's very likely to have happened because the Jericho Road was filled with violent bandits.

> **It's possible that the priest chose to avoid the bloody man so that he wouldn't make himself "unclean" by touching such a battered body.**

As we think about priests and pastors, I'm reminded of my high school basketball coach who was also a pastor. For me, this man was a really good pastor and not just a coach. He paid attention to his players as individuals. He was concerned for their well-being and not just their performance on the court. He was spiritually inclined, but he didn't jam the Bible down the throats of his players. Over the years, I've kept in touch with him here and there. I've always appreciated his deeply rooted concern for people and his awareness of human struggles.

In contrast to my basketball coach, I had another pastor in my educational experience who was abundantly prickly and judgmental. Somehow, he maintained a permanent snarl on his face and disdain oozed from his pores. When people saw this pastor coming toward them, everyone would scurry away to avoid his sarcastic criticism. It's unfortunate, but I could totally see this pastor observing a beat-up human alongside a road and being either disinterested or even repelled by the broken human. I'm sad to say that the priest in Jesus' parable can be experienced in various churches and seminaries in our modern world.

I can think back on various seasons in my life where I've been similar to the priest in the Good Samaritan parable. There have been times when I've seen someone hurting and I didn't want to be bothered with their needs and struggles. There have also been seasons in my life when I figured that a person was in a bad condition because they had made poor decisions, so they needed to learn from the bad consequences. My criticisms and judgments have been unkind and not helpful, devoid of compassion.

Thankfully, God is in the business of redemption and transformation. I'm growing, improving and becoming increasingly compassionate. And it's still interesting to recognize that the priest in the Good Samaritan parable has many modern-day equivalents.

Take some time now to go through the worksheet for this chapter. It could help you to think about the priest in the parable along with what and who that could be in your life.

Priest, Piety and Pity

Almost every religion has a leading religious figure who is responsible for giving advice to adherents. The priest in the parable of the Good Samaritan has a worldview that controls his life, organizes his outlook and defines his values. He is intent on conforming to the religious rigors of his position, and people don't sway his choices, regardless of their condition.

Consider if or how much we might identify with the priest and if we make the same choices with broken people we meet. In thinking about the priest's character, it's possible that our first instincts about identifying with the priest might be revulsion because of the priest's lack of compassion. It's also possible we might relate to the priest and see ourselves making the same choices because people can be messy, confusing, hurtful, or dirty.

1. *Can you think of a time in your life when you were highly devout, meticulous in religious devotion, and rigorous with righteous compliance? What did that look like for you? What defined your choices and priorities in this season?*

2. *During this season in your life, what did your interactions with people look like? Your family? Your friends? Co-workers or classmates?*

3. *Who were your closest friends in this season, and what did your relationship look like with these friends?*

4. *Did you have opportunities to interact with people who were broken, messy, ugly, dysfunctional and/or drastically different from yourself? What did these interactions look like? How did you feel and what did you do and say during these interactions?*

5. *In what ways do you identify with the priest in the Good Samaritan parable?*

6. *In what ways do you find yourself at odds with the priest in this story?*

chapter seven

Levite

"So too, a Levite, when he came to the place
and saw him, passed by on the other side."

LUKE 10:32

Have you ever seen someone being attacked verbally, physically or emotionally and not done anything? I remember one time when I was in my late twenties and visiting a Christian high school, I heard a teacher in the hallway reaming a student. One of the things she said to him really bothered me. "You of all people should know how to behave better since you're the son of the senior pastor of the church for this school. Everyone expects you to behave better and your dad would be ashamed of you today."

As I listened to this teacher attack the student, I was sure that the student had done something wrong, but I was really angry with her using shame and his father's position to berate him. My impulse was to jump into this heated discussion, but I didn't. I listened and watched the student shrink into himself and slink back to class. The teacher held her head up high, maybe thinking that she'd won a moral victory.

What this teacher did was attack the student where he was tender and vulnerable—his relationship with his dad. She didn't speak to the student in relation to his own choices, behavior and integrity. By bringing his dad into the conversation, she closed the door for any dialogue with her student about his choices and his motives for making such choices. Her words and actions poisoned any connection or relationship she might have with this student. And I stood by, watching and listening to all of it, keenly aware of how the student felt, having similar experiences in my upbringing. I was a bystander. I saw the student broken and hurt, but I didn't do anything. I chose to get on with my day rather than stopping to help.

Maybe in this scenario, I was behaving in a similar manner to the Levite in the Good Samaritan parable. This Levite observed the brutalized victim, even came over to see him more closely, and chose to continue walking on the other side of the road. This was the same outcome as the priest we read about in the last chapter. Both men observed the victim but didn't stop to help. They kept walking on their journey. What's the difference between the priest and the Levite?

In the last chapter, we learned about the priest and his very powerful and prominent position in Israel. The Levite was somewhat different from the priest. His religious functions were less visible and revered. Levites were under the supervision of priests, and they were responsible for looking after the music, gates, priest support, upkeep, supply maintenance, and overall functionality of the temple.[12]

This Levite observed the brutalized victim, even came over to see him more closely, and chose to continue walking on the other side of the road.

Additionally, Levites were spread throughout the nation of Israel since this tribe didn't receive a land allotment from Moses when the land of Israel was distributed among the twelve tribes. Instead, the Levites were given more than forty-five cities throughout Israel where they lived to provide religious services in and around these towns. It's interesting to note that Jericho was not one of the original cities designated for Levite habitation.

However, during Jesus' day, Jericho was inhabited by thousands of priests and Levites, so their presence on the Jericho Road wasn't unusual. As for social status during Jesus' day, we could say that priests were the white-collar workers for Judaism in Israel, and Levites were the blue-collar workers for Judaism. Both groups were devoted to religious piety and both groups saw themselves as essential ingredients to maintaining proper worship and religious rigor in their nation. With that in mind, it's not difficult to see how the Levite would walk past the victim on the Jericho Road, just as the priest did.

It can be helpful to understand the dynamics and differences between priests and Levites, but it's also important to think about who the Levites could be in our modern world. Because Levites were associated with worship throughout Israel, a modern equivalent would need to be someone who participates in modern Christianity, possibly an elder, deacon, lay minister or leader, usher, greeter, maybe musicians, various volunteers, small group leader, etc.

For modern churches to be healthy and effective, they need to have lots of people (volunteers, elders, deacons, etc.) to help with the church, ministry, outreaches, and work. I'm a firm proponent of lots of people participating in church for community, getting work done, facilitating outreaches, worship, ministry, and so much more! Indeed, in Ephesians we read, "And He gave some *as* apostles, and some *as* prophets, and some *as* evangelists, and some *as* pastors and teachers, *for the equipping of the saints for the work of service,* to the building up of the body of Christ" (4:11–12 NASB, emphasis added). I firmly believe that Jesus intended for the church to be a community with everyone contributing to the enhancement of the church and world.

But as a lay leader (deacon, elder, usher, musician, small group leader, etc.), we can miss the mark when we fail to engage with people and the needs in our community and around us. If our church titles feed our ego and importance such that we become pristine and haughty, not participating in the lives of messy people, then it's possible that we could be like the Levite in the parable who sees a person who is hurt and gory but just continues along his journey.

Over the course of my life and experiences in church, I've come across a boatload of church volunteers, lay leaders, greeters, small group leaders, etc. Some of the people I've met are nothing less than altogether spectacular. I have a friend in one of the churches where I regularly speak, and he's the sound engineer—such an incredible person! He's always very kind with me and makes it so that the congregation hears a nice blend of music. He helps me when I mess up and doesn't turn on my microphone. I have another friend at a different church who retired from engineering, and he is an essential volunteer at his church, participating in regular board meetings, providing technical support, and is a wise sounding board for his pastor. Truly, I have met some thoroughly amazing and inspiring volunteers in churches and I'm so very honored to get to be with such high-quality people!

> For modern churches to be healthy and effective, they need to have lots of people (volunteers, elders, deacons, etc.) to help with the church, ministry, outreaches and work.

On the other side, I've met lots of church volunteers who have the J&C virus. These individuals are "judgmental and critical," looking down on folk who don't come to church in the right clothes, who might sport some interesting tattoos, who could have body odor, who don't stand or clap during worship, etc. I've also been a part of small groups where an assistant leader has shamed a group member for not knowing a Bible verse or for having human struggles, such as an eating disorder, an addiction, a problem with cussing in the group, chronic use of pornography, or drinking beer or wine with a meal.

Such leaders often use Matthew 7:16 as their justification to express their disapproval. In this verse, Jesus says, *"You will know them by their fruits"* (NASB). The context of this verse is important to consider because Jesus is talking about false prophets who are actually wolves masquerading in sheep's clothing. If we're critical and condemning, it's important to pause and ask if our actions and attitudes reflect and align with Jesus' lifestyle that we see in the Gospels. Furthermore, I think it's very important to honestly ask ourselves if there are times and/or scenarios in which we might be acting similar to the Levite who saw the broken man and decided to keep moving forward with his journey rather than stop and help the injured man.

> **Truly, I have met some thoroughly amazing and inspiring volunteers in churches and I'm so very honored to get to be with such high-quality people!**

As a final reminder, consider that Jesus was telling this parable to a Jewish lawyer who was trying to justify himself. To this end, Jewish priests, Levites and lawyers placed a high level of importance on their devotion to righteous living and conforming to the Mosaic Law with hyper-strict vigilance. They were more concerned about their religious conformity than getting dirty with broken humanity in the journey of their lives.

The lawyer was looking for a legal loophole to justify himself when he asked Jesus, *"Who is my neighbor?"* I think that the priest and Levite in Jesus' parable were also justifying themselves when they walked past the man who was half-dead. As we know, broken people are messy. In contrast, religious people are not as messy, at least on the surface, because of their piety and devotion to righteousness. This brings us to consider if and how much we identify with and behave like the Levite. Let's move over to the worksheet for this chapter to explore some questions about this.

Levites, Lawyers and Legalities

In this parable, the Levite is similar to the priest because they both made the same decision to let the victim stay on the road while they continued their journey. The Levite is a little different from the priest, not only in his religious functions but also in the fact that he came to the victim's location to stop and look.

1. *In what ways could you relate to the Levite?*

2. *Have you had positions in church (deacon, lay leader, usher, small group teacher, greeter, etc.)? What did you do in this/these role(s)?*

3. *Did this role ever conflict with helping someone who was messy, ugly and non-religious? If so, what did that look like? If not, why?*

4. *Some personalities lend themselves to meticulous compliance to social norms and/or religious rigor. Would you consider yourself to have this kind of personality? Why do you answer in the way that you do?*

5. Think of an occasion when you tried to justify yourself, maybe when you felt like you needed to defend yourself in a questionable situation. What was the situation and what did you do/say?

6. How did your actions and words make you feel?

7. If you were to come across a really broken, highly dysfunctional, bloody, messy, and freaky person today, what would you do? How would you feel?

chapter eight

The Innkeeper

An airport hotel can be a great example of a place to pause during a long journey. I haven't stayed at very many airport hotels, maybe just a half dozen, but they're a big improvement over trying to curl up in a quiet corner of an airport for some shut-eye during a long layover. The same holds true for long road trips and staying at a roadside hotel rather than trying to sleep in the car. In thinking about these transit and roadside hotels, they can be a great convenience, but for the victim in the Good Samaritan parable, his stop at the inn along the road was a necessity.

Going from point A to point B is what the traveler sets out to do in the Good Samaritan parable. He leaves Jerusalem and is walking to Jericho. But his journey is interrupted by a violent attack from bandits, so much so that he can't continue his journey without help to recover from the attack. As the Samaritan begins to tend to the traveler, we easily recognize that the traveler needs not only the immediate first aid but also time and ongoing care so that he can fully recover.

In this parable, we read about how the hero took his patient (recovering victim) to an inn so that his healing could continue with more time. The traumatized man needed a place to continue his recovery. The Good Samaritan employed the innkeeper to look after the ongoing healing of the man for whom he was caring. So, the Good Samaritan paid the innkeeper such that the patient had additional time to heal as well as recover.

Generally, I think that the innkeeper is frequently overlooked in this story; however, in his follow-up role to the Good Samaritan, he was really important. If you think about it, the Good Samaritan was like a first responder, seeing the victim, having compassion, engaging, helping, and getting the victim away from the place of trauma. Without the intervention of the hero, the man beaten up on the Jericho Road would remain broken and half-dead. Consequently, the Good Samaritan is a pivotal person in this parable—but the innkeeper is also very important.

What if the Good Samaritan had only done the immediate first aid: binding the wounds and pouring on oil and wine? What if the hero had done these things but left the victim in the place where the trauma had happened? No doubt that the Good Samaritan is the hero of this parable, but the innkeeper is also essential for the man's healing even though he's not as obvious nor active with his care. The innkeeper isn't the first responder, of course, but he is the second person to participate in the victim's recovery. And just because he is second to the first responder doesn't make his role any less important. Indeed, without the continued help from the innkeeper, the efforts of the hero or first responder would be wasted.

I'm bringing this to your attention because trauma recovery isn't just a one-person solution. Just because the Good Samaritan is the obvious hero in this story doesn't mean that the innkeeper is irrelevant. Indeed, the innkeeper is the next person in line to facilitate trauma recovery. To this end, it's important that we see the holistic engagement that Jesus gives in this parable. If the victim of the attack on the Jericho Road is going to experience a full recovery, he needs to have a safe place and time to heal. The Good Samaritan pays the innkeeper to give his patient these essential resources—time, a safe place, rest and room to breathe, pause and reflect.

While you think about recovery being a team experience, let's delve into the world of "innkeeping" during Jesus' day, keeping in mind the importance of hospitality in Middle Eastern culture, that is pretty much timeless. In our modern world, hospitality can have a wide array of expressions. In relation to my house, the hospitality that I offer guests is very laid-back and informal. My pervasive thinking is *mi casa es su casa,* which translates from Spanish to mean, "My house is your house." This line of thinking doesn't really emphasize formality, social etiquette or distance. If you come for dinner at my house, you can expect a tasty meal, time around the kitchen table and maybe a messy environment, like a stack of mail on the counter, coats that need to be hung up and some counter clutter that I often overlook because it's a normal state of existence in my house.

As for Middle Eastern hospitality, this culture is renowned for their extreme efforts to make a guest feel welcome and comfortable. If you are lucky to receive an invitation to dinner at the home of someone in the Middle East, you will likely experience welcome, warmth, time, friendship, conversation, delicious food and a comfortable environment. Hospitality in the Middle East can be seen throughout history, and you can read Genesis 18 to discover Abraham providing hospitality to three angels.

So when the Good Samaritan brings the man beginning his recovery to the inn, there's a lot of unspoken understanding that is assumed by the Good Samaritan. At the inn, the Good Samaritan and the person in his care will receive a safe place to stay, a room and bed for the night, probably breakfast in the morning and maybe dinner for the evening. Of course, the hero will pay for all of this, as is implied with his payment for the future care of his ward, the next morning when he talks with the innkeeper.

But all of this is important to consider not only for the recovery of the trauma victim but also as a resource for the hero. He is moving on to his next thing and is hiring the innkeeper to participate in the ongoing recovery for his patient. It's interesting that Jesus includes the whole innkeeper component into His parable because this tells us that there are participants in the patient's recovery that go past the initial first responder—the Good Samaritan.

When I think about my life and various traumas that I've experienced, I recognize that there have been many heroes or Good Samaritans who have been first responders to engage in the initial steps to help me heal and recover. Additionally, there have also been lots of "innkeepers" in my life who have helped to continue my healing processes from various traumas.

When I was in college, I dislocated my shoulder playing basketball in an intramural game. I sustained this injury because I undercut an opponent who was going for a breakaway layup. I ran into my teammate who was also trying to steal the ball from the opponent, and in the collision, I dislocated my shoulder. Boy did that hurt! Some friends took me to the ER where they gave me morphine before they popped my shoulder back into the socket. But I couldn't stay in the hospital overnight, and I wasn't in any condition to go back to my dorm room.

This is when some "innkeepers" stepped into the picture for me. Some of my college friends had an apartment off campus. They let me crash on their couch through the night, which gave me time to let the morphine tapper off and clear my head so that I could figure out my next steps to recover. I'm grateful for these friends with their sensitivity and generosity. While their help was fairly short, just an overnight stay on their couch, they let me know that I could keep staying with them. They also offered to drive me to any follow-up doctor appointments that I might have. Additionally, they checked in on me every few days over the course of the next weeks. I'm very grateful that these "innkeepers" were part of my healing journey!

There also have been emotional and relational traumas in my life, along with various heroes and innkeepers who contributed to my recovery. Trauma isn't just confined to physical injuries. It's also possible that you could be the trauma victim, and you might be moving to the second phase of recovery. This could be challenging because you might have experienced "trauma bonding" with your Good Samaritan hero. Trauma bonding can be difficult in the journey to recovery. It can also be challenging for the hero. I'm bringing this to your attention because a Good Samaritan can get addicted to the good feelings of helping a person who is recovering from trauma. This can be a set-up for a co-dependent relationship that can stunt full healing from various traumas.

In the journey to recovery, both the victim and hero can relish the immediate uplift that's experienced in the emergency efforts. The hero feels good from the efforts to help, and the victim is relieved from the wound recovery and being lifted away from the place of trauma. So, both the caregiver and victim experience good feelings—and all of us like feeling good!

But for the ongoing healing of the Jericho Road victim, it is essential that he continues on the path of healing. This means that the Good Samaritan first responder must turn over the care of his patient to the innkeeper, who will continue to participate and help with the victim's recovery. Jesus can use lots of different people and methods to heal us from trauma.

Looking at recovery from a different angle, let's consider that you might have been an innkeeper in someone's life who is recovering from trauma. It's possible that you might not have been a first responder—you might have been the "innkeeper" who is the second line of care to help the victim continue to recover. In that role, you are an essential ingredient and participant in someone's recovery.

When I think about it, I have been an innkeeper for various people who were on diverse journeys for healing and recovery. I've had more than a few friends who have struggled with injuries and traumas in their lives, such as domestic abuse, molestation, loss of an important family member, foreclosure, getting fired from a job, accidents, terminal diagnosis, psychological disorders, and childhood injuries. With many of my friends, I haven't been the first responder or Good Samaritan, but I have been an innkeeper to sit with them and participate in their journey to healing. Often times, these journeys take time and go through setbacks.

When we think about the innkeeper, we recognize that at times we need additional help and support. This means that the Good Samaritan isn't the end-all, be-all solution to the patient that he discovered on the Jericho Road. The innkeeper is every bit as important for the victim's recovery.

With this observation, I'd encourage you to reflect on your life and consider the experiences and relationships that could agree with these paradigms: the hero, victim and backup recovery. When you think about these individuals, it's likely that you will see yourself in all three constructs at various times and experiences in your life. So let's move forward into the worksheet for this chapter to do some constructive reflection and application with the innkeeper concept.

Innkeeper

The innkeeper, though not as widely known as the Good Samaritan, was hugely influential in the recovery process for the beaten man. Consider the innkeeper's background role in the story and how you might help other people, even when no one notices.

1. *As a hero or first responder: Is there a time in your life when you were a hero or first responder to someone who was injured physically, mentally or emotionally? How did you feel after this experience? How did it influence your perspective on helping people in times of need?*

2. *As a continuation or innkeeper for someone's recovery from trauma: Describe a time in your life when you were second in line to help someone who was severely injured physically, mentally or emotionally. How did you feel after this experience? How did it influence your perspective on helping people on their recovery journey?*

3. *Friendships and recovery: Have you had friends who have been helpful to you as you healed from trauma? What did they do that was helpful? How did this make you feel? Have you been a friend to someone at various stages of healing from trauma? What did you do that was helpful? How did this make you feel?*

4. *Hesitation or Resistance: Do you have hesitations or hindrances when it comes to helping someone heal from trauma? What might these reservations be? Do you hesitate when it comes to letting someone help you on your journey to heal? What might these reservations be, and why do you have them?*

5. *Trauma bonding: Do you have any experiences with trauma bonding, such that you have been the end-all, be-all for someone getting past trauma? If so, what did you do about this? In your journey to recover from trauma, have you experienced trauma bonding with someone who has helped you on the healing journey? If so, how did you handle this?*

6. *Identifying Innkeepers: Make a list of people who have been "innkeepers" in your life as you recover from trauma. Make a list of people for whom you have been an "innkeeper" on their journey to heal from trauma.*

chapter nine

Do You Want
To Be A Hero?

When Someone is Your Good Samaritan
the verbs part one

Who has been a Good Samaritan to you? I would suppose that maybe you've had a few Good Samaritans in your life, and you have possibly been grateful for them. At first blush, you might think of an occasion when a first responder helped you, such as:

- A paramedic coming to the scene of an accident in which you were involved.

- Someone helping you get into your car
  when you locked your keys in it.

- Someone stopping to help you change a tire.

- A co-worker who took on extra work
  from you during a family crisis.

- A flight attendant being kind and
  helpful when you were sick.

- A classmate who voluntarily tutored you to
  help you get through a difficult class.

I think we've all experienced Good Samaritans in various scenarios and we've probably been really grateful for them! Some Good Samaritans can be quick with their help, and at other times, they can have a longer runway. But no matter what, the world is a better place for Good Samaritans regardless of the time duration, intensity of their help, personal connection, location or season of life.

Usually the hero of the parable gets the most attention, and understandably so. In this chapter and the next, we will look at the verbs in this parable from two angles—the hero and the patient/victim. My goal for you is to see yourself from both perspectives and thereby engage with these verbs from these different points of view. In this chapter, we will look at people who are Good Samaritans and what their actions are.

Have you experienced a situation where someone was a Good Samaritan to you, maybe helping to heal wounds, pains, traumas that you've experienced? As I mentioned earlier, first responders are often seen as the proverbial Good Samaritan because of their participation in responding to a crisis injury and providing immediate support and first aid.

I'd like to suggest, however, that Good Samaritans can include not just the first responder or paramedic type person but other people. For example, I have some friends, a married couple who are normal people, a retired salesman and retired teacher. I've known this couple for a few decades, and over the course of time, I've seen them be Good Samaritans on many occasions. For all practical purposes, this couple has been surrogate parents to lots of teenagers and young adults.

I would suppose that maybe you've had a few Good Samaritans in your life, and you have possibly been grateful for them.

In one situation, they let a high school girl move in with them for all of her education and for some years after high school so that she could get her feet under her. This girl came from a pretty broken home that had lots of dysfunction, instability, harmful scenarios and jagged edges. My friends saw that this girl was really struggling and on the cusp of drowning. They had compassion, offered their home as a safe refuge, and gave her not only lodging and time but also healthy interactions and conversations so that she could heal, recover and successfully move onto the next chapter of her life.

In watching this couple, I've seen them do this Good Samaritan behavior with lots of broken and wounded teens and young adults over the course of a few decades. I'd venture to say that they've been Good Samaritans to more than a dozen people, including myself, and I'm deeply honored to know them. Of course, they aren't perfect, and they've had more than their share of heartbreak and struggles, but in terms of being Good Samaritans, maybe they're the best examples that I know.

But no matter what, the world is a better place for Good Samaritans regardless of the time duration, intensity of their help, personal connection, location or season of life.

What are the actions that could qualify us to be Good Samaritans? To answer this question, we need to look at the actions that the hero took in this parable. We need to reflect and digest these verbs.

In this parable, the hero employs eight verbs. He also invests two things to facilitate the healing and recovery of his "patient." Let's look at these verbs and make some observations as to how they're used in the Greek language. This will help us to explore some essential insights and applications of what it looks like to participate in someone else's trauma recovery. As a quick overview, these are the actions the Good Samaritan took as well as the associated Greek word:

English verbs:	Greek:
To see	ὁράω
To have compassion	σπλαγχνίζομαι
To come	προσέρχομαι
To bind	καταδέω
To pour	ἐπιχέω
To lift	ἐπιβιβάζω
To lead	ἄγω
To take care of	ἐπιμελέομαι

The two investments that the Good Samaritan uses are *money* and *time*. "*On the next day he took out two denarii and gave them to the innkeeper and said, 'Take care of him; and whatever more you spend, when I return I will repay you'*" (Luke 10:35 NASB). From this verse, we see that the Good Samaritan gave the innkeeper money to look after his patient. The money he gave the innkeeper was to buy the time and the care his patient needed to recover. The dude that was beat up needed all of the above actions as well as the time and money so that he could continue to heal.

Let's take some moments to think about each verb and what that could look like for us as we participate in the recovery of those who have experienced trauma.

ὁράω—to see

The first verb that starts the recovery journey is the verb ὁράω (horao) or to see. In the Greek, this verb is different than the sister verb, βλέπω (blepo), which also means to see. The difference between these verbs is that *blepo* is more of a quick look or glance and *horao* is to look with attention or to observe with understanding. If we are going to be Good Samaritans to those who have experienced trauma, the first requirement is that we *see* the person and not just the trauma. When we think about this verb, it's interesting to note that not only did the Good Samaritan *see* the man who was badly beaten on the Jericho Road, but the priest and Levite also saw the same victim. In the next verb, we'll consider the difference between the Good Samaritan and these religious leaders.

If we are going to be Good Samaritans to those who have experienced trauma, the first requirement is that we *see* the person and not just the trauma.

For a modern example of what it means to *see* someone, I reference my friends that I gave as examples of Good Samaritans at the beginning of this chapter. In their various interactions with helping people who are victims of trauma, they are very skilled at seeing beyond the trauma to the person. They recognize that dysfunction, addictive behaviors, ugly choices and hateful words are byproducts of previous trauma. At the same time, they don't let the ugly side of a person's trauma have unbounded access. My friends see the person and not just the trauma.

σπλαγχνίζομαι—to have compassion

The next action of the Good Samaritan is to have compassion. This is the stark and fundamental difference between the hero in this parable and the religious leaders (priest and Levite) or bystanders. All three travelers on the Jericho Road observed the half-dead victim. But only the Good Samaritan, the hero of the story, had compassion for the badly beaten man. If we are religious, pious and "good Christians," we should continue to keep compassion as our essential lens through which we see people and victims of trauma. If we don't have compassion, then we can easily turn into the priest or Levite who see broken people but just go on their way.

So what does it mean to have compassion? What does this word mean in the Greek, and how is it used in the New Testament? Everywhere this verb is used in the New Testament, it is attributed to or closely associated with Jesus and His interactions with people.

In the Greek, this verb means to have pity, deep feeling or visceral attention for someone—to feel deeply even into one's kidneys, heart and inner organs. This word also has deep roots in the Old Testament and can be seen with the Hebrew equivalent word, *raccham*. Consider the description of God in Psalm 145. *"The LORD is gracious and compassionate, slow to anger and rich in love"* (v. 8, NIV).

I have seen my friends employ their compassionate lens for victims of trauma on more than one occasion. They have an uncanny, maybe even supernatural ability, to look past the ugly of trauma and see the wounded person who is in desperate need of compassion and healing.

προσέρχομαι—to come

After looking at the Jericho victim with compassion, the Good Samaritan comes to the beaten man. While this might not seem like anything significant, I bring this verb to your attention because if you're like me, we could be repelled by trauma rather than moving close to it. I can make up all kinds of reasons and excuses to walk away from or ignore trauma victims. We talked about this in an earlier chapter, but if we are truly going to be Good Samaritans, then we have to forego our excuses and justifications to pass over victims of trauma. The hero of this parable came to the victim. He stopped his journey and made space to help the beaten man.

I've often seen my friends *come to* a victim of trauma and participate in their recovery. The various ways that they've come alongside a wounded person are by letting that person sit with them in church every Sunday, steadily inviting the person for meals at their home, letting the person stay with them for a defined season, and giving the person meals and conversation, among many other things. My friends *come* to trauma victims in lots of different ways.

καταδέω—to bind

Upon coming to the beaten man on the Jericho Road, the Good Samaritan *binds* the wounds (or trauma) of this man. In Greek, this word means to enclose a wound. In a modern context, it would be akin to putting a bandage on a wound. But what's really important to consider is that the Good Samaritan didn't just put a cursory Band-Aid on a half dead man. The hero of this parable did total wound care, including pouring oil and wine into the cuts. We'll talk about that more in the next section. But the emphasis here is that the Good Samaritan participated in the victim's recovery, and he did the practical things to facilitate healing.

My friends have also *bound up the wounds* of many trauma victims. They have sat with people who are coming off a bender, listening to blather and nonsense. They have listened to more than a little bit of crazy coming from trauma-deranged victims, and they have made hundreds of pots of coffee to help people along their journey to healing.

ἐπιχέω—to pour

In the parable, the hero pours oil and wine onto the wounds of the trauma victim on the Jericho Road. This word *pour*, along with *bind*, in Greek are only used in this parable in the New Testament—it is found nowhere else in the Bible. I'd suggest to you that Luke, the author of this Gospel and also a doctor, had a keen appreciation for medical concerns and healing. He gave details to communicate the specific treatments needed for the victim's healing. Luke tells us that the hero disinfected and soothed the victim's wounds with oil. Before our modern-day Neosporin, the Good Samaritan had to do two *pourings* rather than a singular administration of antiseptic cream.

The importance of these actions is that the hero cleansed the wounds so that they wouldn't get infected and make the man's half-dead condition even worse. Additionally, the oil was soothing and calming to the wounds that were painful, tender and angry. In trauma care, antiseptics and soothing are necessary teammates.

I see my friends also employ these tactics in how they come alongside various victims of trauma. They are committed to cleansing the wounds from trauma, administering truth, challenging deceptions and acknowledging people's failures. At the same time, they give comfort and hope by pointing their patients to Jesus and helping them see Jesus' love for them.

ἐπιβιβάζω—to lift up

Not only does the Good Samaritan look after the wounds/traumas of the Jericho Road traveler, but he also lifts him up and sets him on his beast of burden. Clearly, the brutalized man couldn't walk, so it's noteworthy to see that the hero's beast of burden was used to provide transportation to this broken victim. In the New Testament, this word is used two other times: when the donkey carried Jesus into Jerusalem on His triumphal entry

(Palm Sunday) and when Paul was brought to Felix, the Roman Governor at Caesarea.

As this relates to my friends, I have seen them on countless occasions *lift up* a trauma victim. They help get their focus upward rather than being controlled and defined by trauma. When a person is brutally traumatized, it can be difficult for them to get up or see that they don't have to die as a victim of the trauma that has happened to them. I love that my friends help to dislodge people from being stuck in trauma.

ἄγω—to lead or to bring

Upon getting the Jericho Road traveler on his beast of burden, the Good Samaritan leads him away from the trauma and gets this traveler further along his journey, even though he's half dead. In Greek, this word ἄγω is extremely common and is used almost seventy times in the New Testament. Because it is so frequently used, there are a variety of applications. In the most simple and reliable usage, however, it means to lead or bring.

I also see my friends do this leading/bringing along with various trauma victims that they have helped. One of the things I love about my friends is that they will help a person to move away from the trauma that they've experienced. The victim needs to be willing to participate with that journey. Unfortunately, not everyone wants to leave the trauma that they've experienced, and many people grow accustomed to the dysfunction and coping methods that can be very hurtful and destructive. Heroes can help as much as they are allowed to help.

ἐπιμελέομαι—to take care of

Having brought the traumatized traveler to an inn, the Good Samaritan *takes care of* his patient. This word in Greek isn't commonly found in either ancient Greek literature nor in the New Testament, so it's pretty straightforward. Its meaning is literally to take care of, pay attention to or be mindful of. We could understand this to mean that the Good Samaritan takes his patient to a room at the inn, continues to look after him through the night, attends to troublesome and painful wounds, helps his patient to be comfortable, makes sure that he has water and food as he's able to ingest, and helps him to sleep.

My friends have also done more than their share of *taking care* of trauma victims over the years. They've looked after young adults who have lived with them, listened to pain-filled histories, attended to the wounds that often creep up and re-appear as a person heals from trauma, and they've given soothing and restorative care to many people.

Two Investments: Money and Time

As we come to the end of this parable, I want to again draw your attention to two investments that the Good Samaritan leaves for his trauma patient to continue his recovery. We read that he pays the innkeeper two denarii to allow the recovering traveler to stay and continue to mend (Luke 10:35). In essence, the hero buys time so that his patient can move forward on his healing journey. It's interesting to consider that there are two journeys in this parable—the physical journey the traveler takes as he begins to walk to Jericho and the healing journey that is facilitated by the Good Samaritan. Both journeys require time and money, but one journey is drastically more personal and transforming.

My friends have invested time, money and friendship to see people move forward on various journeys to healing. On more than one occasion, I've talked with my friends about their relationships that are like the Good Samaritan. In one of my conversations, they made this thought-provoking observation. "Sarah, the most overlooked person in this parable is the innkeeper. He plays a distant cameo role in the parable, but he is still a vital component for the patient's recovery. No one person, except Jesus, is the end-all, be-all, cure-all for victims of trauma. We can all play a role, be that as a first responder or a follow-up caretaker. All of us can participate in helping a person recover from trauma."

Think again about the actions or verbs that the Good Samaritan employed when he came across the victim suffering from trauma. We can be heroes, or partial heroes, for people who have been traumatized. Let's remember these actions as necessary ingredients for our hero toolbox. Those actions are seeing, having compassion, coming to, bandaging, pouring, lifting, leading, and taking care of, along with the two investments (money and time). The worksheet for this chapter can help you think about how to use these actions and improve your hero potential.

Hero Actions

Verbs:

to see	to have compassion	to come
to bind/bandage	to pour	to lift up
to lead	to take care of	

In thinking about the verbs or actions that the Good Samaritan used, answer the following questions:

1. *Which verb is most natural and easiest for you to do? Why?*

2. *Which verb is most difficult for you to do? Why?*

3. *Which of these verbs do you most frequently use and in what context? Could you see yourself using this verb in different contexts? In what other contexts could you use this verb?*

4. *Do you think of these verbs as a sequence? Is that a rigid order for you? Why or why not?*

5. *Using a few of these verbs, describe a time when you were a Good Samaritan and helped someone in need. How did that make you feel?*

6. Describe a time when you saw someone in need but didn't stop to help. How did that make you feel?

7. Are there situations when you should not stop to help someone? Describe your thinking.

8. What do you consider to be your weakest area or ability with being a Good Samaritan?

9. What are your thoughts about the Good Samaritan spending money for the man's continued recovery?

chapter ten

When You Suffer From Trauma

Recognizing Trauma
the verbs part two

As we come to the last chapter in this book, let's look at the journey you can take to recover from trauma. We will consider the verbs that the traveler experienced at the hands of the Good Samaritan so that he could recover and heal, using this context for our own trauma recovery journey.

In the previous chapter, we explored how to employ the verbs the hero used to facilitate healing for his patient. In this chapter, we'll look at how we can experience these actions so that we move forward to heal from traumas that have happened to us. The effects of traumatic experiences can be difficult to work through. We don't want to get stuck in trauma and remain half dead.

I'm very keen about acknowledging and recognizing trauma because of my own ignorance and denial for many years. I think that most of us can identify stuff in our past that has been hurtful and difficult to navigate, but maybe we don't recognize the impact and ripples such things have on our outlook, priorities, relationships, conversations, etc. Additionally, you may have blocked out some hurts from the past so that you can be functional in the present. In this scenario, it's possible that you don't understand why you do what you do nor what influences your perspective and values. Maybe we think:

- It's not that bad—no big deal.

- That happened a long time ago—it's a non-issue.

- Those experiences are too horrific to overcome.

- I have to live in the constructs of my trauma. I'm stuck and can't get away.

- When I get to heaven, I won't have to deal with any of this pain. I must endure the present to get to a better future.

- What I experienced isn't as bad as what other people have suffered—minimizing by comparison.

- I've learned how to cope with the trauma— possibly using unhealthy coping mechanisms.

- The person who inflicted pain in my life wasn't that bad. They loved me and did their best—justifying the abuse/neglect.

All of these responses only serve to minimize, dismiss, ignore, belittle and deny trauma. From first-hand experience, let me say that such strategies are neither helpful nor healing. If you're like me, you might think that ignoring traumas from your past will give that stuff time to heal. Focusing on it now is like picking a scab and creating opportunities for infection and more pain. Let bygones be bygones and get on with your life. That was my perspective for many decades. Until the bygones crept into my present, and I began to recognize the sabotage that trauma was causing me.

We don't want to get stuck in trauma and remain half dead.

Regardless of what you experienced, be it horrific or seemingly minor, I sincerely believe that Jesus wants you to live in health and freedom from the effects and constrictions of the past that's been informed by trauma. So, let's look at the verbs employed by the Good Samaritan and see how they relate to us as the brutalized victim on the Jericho Road, maybe stuck and trapped in trauma. As a quick reminder, these are the actions the Good Samaritan took and the equivalent Greek word:

English verbs: **Greek:**

To see.................................ὁράω

To have compassion...............σπλαγχνίζομαι

To come ....προσέρχομαι

To bind..................................καταδέω

To pour ....ἐπιχέω

To lift ....ἐπιβιβάζω

To lead ....ἄγω

To take care of......................ἐπιμελέομαι

Let's look at each verb and consider what that means for us as we move along our journey to recover from wounds and traumas.

ὁράω—to see

In thinking about this verb as it relates to recovering from trauma, I'd like to suggest that we won't heal from the traumas that we've experienced until we first look at and acknowledge things that have hurt us—injuries that have left us impaired and crippled. As an example, I'm reminded of a friend who was entirely incapable of any kind of public speaking. She even told me once that she'd rather lose her job than do any kind of speaking in public. When I asked her why this was such an obstacle for her, she explained that in second grade, her teacher had whacked her knuckles with a ruler when she was at the chalkboard in front of the room and explaining a math problem on the board. Thankfully, my friend was aware of the roots of her resistance to public speaking, but she hadn't done anything beyond that awareness.

As we think about this verb as a starting point for our journey to recover from pains and traumas in our past, we should not only observe what's happened to us in the past, but we should also let others see or be aware of what has happened to us. This idea runs contrary to modern American culture, that heralds the uber-achievers and hyper-confident success. Indeed, maybe we look for these kinds of flawless and invincible ideals so that we don't have to think about or sit in the pain of our traumas. But recovery and healing doesn't happen because we let ourselves be distracted. Focus and truth are essential ingredients for our healing.

Of course, not everyone who sees you as a victim on the Jericho Road is going to participate in your recovery. Remember that two of the three people who saw the brutalized man did nothing and kept walking. Some people in your life won't participate in your recovery. Be careful, however, that the behaviors of such people don't cause you to hide and disguise the trauma that you're dealing with. Being authentically seen for the ugliness of what has happened to you is an essential ingredient on the journey to healing and recovery.

σπλαγχνίζομαι—to have compassion

Another action of the Good Samaritan that's important for a trauma victim is compassion. The absence of compassion facilitates the vigilance of protection. Of course, it's important to protect ourselves, and that's usually a hardwired instinct in our souls. But protecting ourselves from compassion will not help us to recover from trauma.

So what could compassion look like as we think about healing? I would suggest that compassion can be experienced not only externally, from others, but also internally. We can choose to be gentle with ourselves rather than harsh, critical, condemning, degrading and judgmental. The self-talk that goes on in our thoughts is something that we should consider. Think about a few adjustments to some thoughts that might go through your mind:

- I screwed up, but I'm not a screwup.

- I failed, but I'm not a failure.

- I lost, but I'm not a loser.

- I didn't get the job or accepted to the school, but that doesn't prevent or sabotage my success.

- I'm loved by God no matter my achievements, failures, accolades, or depravity.

- When I hurt, it's better to be gentle
  with myself rather than harsh.

- Patience is an important cousin to compassion.

- Even though I haven't arrived, I'm not where I started.

I'd also suggest that compassion from people around us can be an important ingredient as we heal from the trauma that we've experienced. I'm coming to recognize and appreciate compassion that I receive from people around me. There have been innumerable times when people have been patient with me as I've stumbled and fumbled to keep up, do my job, be productive, and contribute as a team member. I've also received compassion in the form of forgiveness when I've screwed up and didn't meet an expectation. Additionally, I've experienced compassion when people see that I'm inadequate and struggling with insecurity along with other ripples and residues of trauma.

We can choose to be gentle with ourselves rather than harsh, critical, condemning, degrading and judgmental.

When I think about compassion, I'm reminded of the famous quote from the movie *The Help*. "You is kind, you is smart, you is important."[13] This is what the African American maid/nanny, Aibileen, says to the little girl, Mae Mobley, who is continually berated and criticized by her mom. Trauma tells us that we are unkind, stupid, ugly and irrelevant. Compassion interrupts that narrative with the gentle truth that is informed with divine love: You is kind, you is wise and you is important.

προσέρχομαι—to come

The third verb to think about on our journey in trauma recovery relates to letting others come to us or get close. I'd suggest that this can possibly be a challenge when we are in the throes and consequences of trauma. Indeed, when we hurt, it's not uncommon to hunker down and protect ourselves from people, since people have been the perpetrators of pain.

In the Good Samaritan parable, however, the hero comes to the victim who had been badly beaten and left half dead. This important verb reminds us that we don't heal from trauma in isolation or exclusion. At the same time, we need to recognize that Jesus can orchestrate our healing by using people. Most importantly, though, we receive His healing by letting Him come to us in our painful, brutalized and trauma-infested existence.

καταδέω/ἐπιχέω—to bind/to pour

As we continue the journey of healing from traumas, I'm going to combine two verbs that are intricately related: to bind and to pour. Before bandaging or binding traumas, we must disinfect and soothe the injuries so that healing can be experienced. We need to let the wounds of the past be cleaned and disinfected so that they don't fester, get infected or compromise our healing. Getting out the dirt from a wound can mean practicing forgiveness, releasing bitterness, letting go of painful memories and washing away the debt owed to you from the pain that was inflicted on you. Additionally, truth can be a powerful and restorative antiseptic to counteract the infections that can fester from deceptions that often accompany trauma.

Of course, it is important to clean a wound that we've experienced, but it's equally important to bind or cover that wound so that it can remain clean and have room to heal. Remember, however, that a Band-Aid (covering a wound) is only effective if the wound has been cleaned. Covering without cleaning doesn't facilitate healing. As for covering or binding a wound, this is when we actively choose not to let past wounds control our present choices or perspectives.

We need to let the wounds of the past be cleaned and disinfected so that they don't fester, get infected or compromise our healing.

I've come to recognize various wounds from my past and their possible impact on me. I've chosen to forgive the people who have wounded me, and I actively choose, with God's help, not to let those wounds bleed into my conversations, interactions or outlook. I'm learning that healing from trauma requires antiseptic (cleaning), oil (soothing) and bandaging (covering and protection). For all of this, I find that Jesus is the best doctor and therapist, along with loving friends and possibly some insightful counselors.

ἐπιβιβάζω—to lift up

It is critically important that we choose to let ourselves be lifted up or extracted from the place(s) and experiences associated with trauma. Remaining in the place where trauma has occurred can be detrimental to our healing and recovery. Additionally, going back to similar experiences and relationships that have familiar trauma contexts for us should be carefully and prayerfully evaluated. The same can be said for unhealthy methods that we've used to cope with trauma, such as substance abuse, addictions and distractions. Whatever keeps us stuck or trapped in trauma is unhealthy, and we would be wise to ask Jesus to lift us out of the trauma quagmire.

ἄγω—to lead or to bring

In addition to being lifted from the place of trauma, let's also recognize that we need to journey away from that place. To move forward in healing from trauma, we need to value the process and the journey. As I think about this important verb, I'm reminded of various places, relationships and contexts through which I've experienced trauma. As I continue to heal, I find myself actively choosing to stay away from such things and people. Because I'm on a healing journey, I am responsible to employ healthy boundaries, to be wise and to recognize that I'm not invincible or impervious to trauma and pain.

I know that I have tender spots and vulnerabilities to various traumas. I recognize that these tender spots come from the past, and I actively choose to keep letting Jesus move me away from these wounds because I'm on a healing journey with Him. I've come to realize that I can't stay in certain scenarios and be healthy, nor can I continue to suffer from the effects of trauma that have been crippling to me in the past. While it would be fantastic to have an immediate and miraculous healing from trauma, and sometimes that happens, more often I see that healing is a journey and process. On occasion, we have setbacks along that journey, but let's remain committed to progress and not just be discouraged when we have struggles along the way.

ἐπιμελέομαι—to take care of

The final verb from the Good Samaritan parable brings us to the idea of care and nurture. Care and nurture are essential ingredients for healing from trauma. At the same time, it can be difficult for us to receive care and nurture when we've employed layers of protection and shielding so that the wounds from trauma don't get triggered or touched. Nevertheless, to live in healing from trauma, we must let Jesus take care of and nurture us. It is not uncommon for Jesus to use various people in our lives for such care and nurturing.

As I think about the importance of this verb, I think about some of my friends who have walked with me along this healing journey. Some of my friends have been abundantly patient and gracious with me, extending forgiveness and understanding. Other friends have both laughed and cried with me at various points on this path. I also know that some of my friends have been with me just for a season or for a specific reason, but not necessarily for the long haul. I also hope that all of them would say that I have been a fellow traveler with them on their own healing journey from trauma, such that our relationship is mutual and not just one-sided. Taking care of people and being taken care of by people are necessary ingredients to recover from trauma. Sometimes this is easier said than done.

> **Care and nurture are essential ingredients for healing from trauma. …it can be difficult for us to receive care and nurture when we've employed layers of protection and shielding so that the wounds from trauma don't get triggered or touched.**

I recognize that time and money were used by the Good Samaritan to help his patient recover from trauma. I believe these elements are also necessary for our own healing journey. It can take both time and money to heal from the debilitating effects of trauma. I want to encourage you to be patient with yourself as you recover, and I urge you to consider investing in counseling to help you work through issues. Be kind to yourself.

Finally, please remember that Jesus is a man acquainted with and well experienced with human trauma.

He was despised and forsaken of men, a man of sorrows and acquainted with grief; and like one from whom men hide their face He was despised, and we did not esteem Him. Surely our griefs He Himself bore, and our sorrows He carried; yet we ourselves esteemed Him stricken, smitten of God, and afflicted. But He was pierced through for our transgressions, He was crushed for our iniquities; the chastening for our well-being fell upon Him, and by His scourging we are healed (Isaiah 53:3–5 NASB).

In conclusion, I know that Jesus has used various people in my life as I move along the journey to healing from trauma. Most importantly, I know that Jesus loves me deeply and is healing me from the wounds in my past, regardless of humans who are or are not in my life. I know this to be true for you too. Jesus loves you deeply and wants to walk by your side on your journey to healing!

The Healing Journey

Verbs:

to see	to have compassion	to come
to bind/bandage	to pour	to lift up
to lead	to take care of	

In thinking about the verbs or actions that the trauma victim on the Jericho Road experienced, answer the following questions:

1. *Describe a situation in your life where you were like the trauma victim on the Jericho Road. How did this situation affect your outlook, choices and values?*

2. *What could be the trauma ripples in your life from this situation? This is similar to the second part of question one. Think about, identify and assess what impact this has on your life.*

3. *Which verb is most natural and easiest for you to receive? Why?*

4. *Which verb is most difficult for you to receive or experience? Why?*

5. *Which of these verbs have you experienced to help you recover from trauma? Give an example for each verb that you identify.*

6. *Which of these verbs have you not experienced or minimally experienced such that they are deficient in your recovery from trauma? Think about and explain why each of these verbs might be missing or minimally experienced.*

7. *How do you see God in relation to your trauma experience?*

8. *How do you see God in relation to your recovery journey from trauma?*

9. *How do you feel and what do you think about these ingredients that could accompany your healing and recovery from trauma?*

   forgiveness:

   boundaries:

   friendships:

   acquaintances:

   time:

   hurts:

   choices you make:

   truth:

   trust:

chapter eleven

Where Do I Go From Here?

As we come to the end of this book, we should look back on what we've learned. We've considered the various characters in the Good Samaritan parable, and we've discussed ways in which we might be similar or share some commonality with each character. We've also looked at various people in our lives, thinking about how individuals could have been one or a combination of the individuals in this parable. At the end of all of these reflections, we need to make some conclusions about trauma because it's a universal human experience.

To begin, every human sets out as a traveler on the journey of life. Along this journey, we come across broken people, pious folk, helpers, people who are indifferent, healers and fellow travelers—just like the characters in the parable. Furthermore, on this journey, we have been pious, hurtful, busy, apathetic, injured, helpful and neutral travelers. We all have been the various individuals in this parable at different junctures, seasons and occasions in our lives. It's important for us to recognize that we have been, and maybe we currently are, at least one of the individuals in the Good Samaritan parable.

In the midst of all of these characters, I'd like for you to think about your own traumas and consider how you've navigated these pains. Sometimes, we do fairly well with these traumas, and we make good progress for healing and recovery. At other times, we don't do so well and can get stuck in the trauma quagmire. Additionally, we can probably see others who are struggling with the impact of trauma, and hopefully, we can have compassion and grace for their journey and challenges.

To begin, every human sets out as a traveler on the journey of life.

Over the course of this book, it is my prayer that you have become aware of trauma in your life, and I hope that you can see it more easily in the lives of others. This is important because each of us is walking a road that is difficult, regardless if others recognize our struggles. Just because you can't see or understand the internal struggles of another person doesn't make their difficulties irrelevant.

Progress over Destination

On the journey to recovery and healing, we all want to reach the final destination. We want to stop hurting, and we want for ourselves and the people we love to be healthy. Maybe we want to be free from the past and experiences that have resulted in trauma that we continue to navigate.

I'd like to suggest that progress is both necessary and helpful. I know that we want to arrive at our destination of healing often times without having to navigate pain or trauma. Not only do we need this for ourselves, but we also want this for the people we love.

Let's acknowledge and celebrate progress, even though we haven't reached our destination or resolved the pain and trauma that we've experienced. While the people we love (including ourselves), haven't reached their final destination, let's be satisfied with progress before we reach our destination.

Pause over Speed

When we think about the Good Samaritan parable, it's important to look at the "pause" that the victim/traveler experienced along his journey. I think this is important to consider because our modern existence is very much conditioned to value speed over pause. We want instant gratification and fulfillment, so we neglect pause and process.

In this parable, time (including pause) was an integral ingredient for everyone, maybe most of all the traveler on the Jericho

Road. With this observation, let's be careful that speed doesn't become more important than healing and recovery. Don't be impatient.

Truth over Deception

Truth is an essential antidote for deception. Religion doesn't always include nor embrace truth. Indeed, religion can circumvent truth and pretend to be its counterfeit.

In the Good Samaritan parable, truth and deception become murky in the contexts of religion, piety and obligation. If we are going to heal from trauma, we need to accentuate truth even when it's at the expense of deception and perceived healing.

Image over Warts

The problem with image is that it's a perceived attraction rather than an actual reality. We have a pursuit for image rather than reality and flaws. Many times, the image smokescreen can disguise trauma and prevent healing and recovery.

While the image delusion isn't explicit in the Good Samaritan parable, it is nonetheless a modern reality that doesn't facilitate healing from trauma.

Relationship over Religion

In Jesus' Good Samaritan story, we see that He prioritizes relationship over religion. Read again what He says about the priest and

Levite in this parable. Indeed, the only person who is relational in this story is the Good Samaritan. The religious participants are nothing more than spectators.

It's important that we remember this value so that religion doesn't become a continuation of the trauma that we've experienced. Let's keep in mind that God is wholly relational as expressed in His triune nature. God is Trinity. Religion leaves us as a victim of trauma, but relationship helps us move away from and heal from trauma.

Growing over Stagnation

The contrast between growth and stagnation is tied to the victim growing and moving away from the place where he experienced trauma. This is important because growth is an indicator that we aren't stuck or trapped in the trauma that we've experienced. In contrast, stagnation is an indication that we are stuck in trauma.

Thankfully, Jesus gives us this parable to show that we can grow, move away and heal from trauma that has happened to us. No doubt that this is a journey that includes setbacks and struggles, but recovery and healing from trauma is possible, and we can walk with Jesus in this process.

In the movie "Finding Nemo," Dori tells Nemo that if he keeps swimming, he will make it to his goal. In our lives, Jesus tells us to keep walking with Him and we can experience healing and redemption! Keep walking!

Intermission

I'm really excited to break this book into two parts. The first part, which you just read, walks you through Jesus' parable on trauma and recovery. I firmly believe that Jesus gave us this parable so that we can be aware of trauma, its effects on our lives, and being conscious of people in our lives who are navigating various effects of trauma as well. No doubt, the Bible can be very helpful and healing!

In the second part of this book, you will read a modern rendition of this parable. Because this allegory is set in our present world, you'll note that it has some very strong descriptions and challenging interviews that could be disturbing. As a reader, you might be unsettled or even triggered by some of the content in this rendition of the Good Samaritan parable. That's the problem with trauma—it's disturbing, upsetting and sometimes even triggering.

Nevertheless, the allegory that you're about to read will help you see what the respective characters in the Good Samaritan parable could look like in our modern world. More importantly, I hope that you might find some help in this fiction to possibly see yourself (or parts of yourself) in each character.

I'm also very proud to co-write this book with my daughter, Isabell Bowling. She's such a wise, bright, compassionate and exceptional person! It's nothing more than my greatest delight to write this book with her and to capitalize on our respective strengths. She has written this allegory to the Good Samaritan parable so that you could see what this would look like today, possibly where you live and in your life.

Warning: Some scenes, language and content in this allegory have the potential to trigger or evoke strong emotions in a reader, possibly stirring up memories that have been hurtful. It is our prayer that you will experience the comfort, healing and redemption of the Holy Spirit in your soul to transform traumas that you may have experienced and the ripple effects that could be impacting your life today.

Let's jump into our modern allegory of the Good Samaritan and explore God's redeeming process!

ROAD TO WHOLENESS

part two

chapter one

The Journalist

Love does not delight in evil but rejoices with the truth.

1 CORINTHIANS 13:6

My stomach turned, and the coffee I had guzzled down earlier threatened to make a reappearance.

"Julie?" The nurse looked at me. "Are you okay?"

I swallowed hard and turned my head away. "Yep," I responded.

The body that lay before me had been brutally attacked. No question about it; this was the work of the POTG club. The man, who was sleeping, had a broken jaw, and the lower half of his body was swathed in thick, white bandages. The nurse told me that his attacker had attempted to castrate him.

Here's the thing: This man deserved it. In all my research, all my questioning, I had learned that this club rarely did anything without a "moral" reason. This scumbag had a rap sheet a mile long, full of rape, domestic violence and abuse. I had read the police report. In one interview, he claimed that his victim had "enjoyed every minute."

The man shifted his body, and I started. He was restrained, but my heart still started pounding a little harder. The nurse walked over to my side of the bed and wrapped her arm around me. She began to walk me out, and I followed her. I had come to the local hospital to interview this "victim," but he was asleep. So, a waste of a journey.

"Are you okay?" she asked again.

I paused. "No," I responded. "I have a deadline on this story, and every lead I follow is a dead end. I need a win!"

The nurse paused. I sensed that there was something she wasn't saying, so I waited. In all my time as an investigative reporter, I've learned to wait out the truth because it always finds me.

"There's a woman . . ." she began. "We discharged her yesterday, and she was looking for reporters to talk to. But I can't officially tell you anything about her."

"I understand . . ." I said, waiting with a pregnant pause.

"Her name is Molly," the nurse finally said, "and that's all I can tell you."

My heart leapt, but I maintained decorum and shook her hand.

"Thank you," I looked at her name badge, "Mary."

In the next five minutes, I called my contact at the police department and got a verbal report on Molly, who had been rushed to the hospital about a week ago. I ran by the police station and picked up her file.

What I read played out like a bad cliché. This poor girl had been suffering abuse for years. When she was a child, CPS had removed her from her parents' custody, and she had grown up in foster homes. She had a history of promiscuity, and her first prostitution charge was when she was fifteen. Things didn't get much better from there. She had been fined for prostitution multiple times and had done community service last year. She had also bailed out countless guys who were in on drug charges, and this latest attack on her wasn't the first time she had been in the hospital. But this was by far the most brutal.

This was going to be a tricky interview. This woman had experienced a lifetime of trauma, and I wanted to be careful with how hard I pushed her. I didn't want to add to her struggles. I needed to call in the big guns, so I called my grandfather.

"*Hi, Pops!*" I yelled into the phone.

"*Hi, Sugar!*" he responded, equally as loudly. "How can I help you?"

Pops had won a Pulitzer Prize back in the day, and whenever I had a tricky writing project, I called him. He was elderly and half deaf, but still sharp as a tack.

"Pops, I'm about to ask a woman for an interview, but she might not want to talk to me. She has been brutalized by that horrible club, and I'm trying to report on her attackers. I don't want to add to her trauma. How can I protect her and still get the story I need?"

"That's a great question," he answered. "First off, I would conduct the interview in her house, if possible. You want her to feel she has as much control as she needs. Secondly, offer to use an alias instead of her name. It's possible that her attackers threatened her family."

I was jotting down notes as he spoke, an old habit, and his last comment made me pause. *What if the POTG club knows who I am and what I'm doing?* I wondered. *Will they come after my family? Am I safe?*

I had asked myself these questions before, but for some reason, hearing my grandfather talk about the possibility made it all the more real for me. What I was doing was dangerous. But this club had been terrorizing Smythville for too long. This story was too important.

"Is there anything else I need to know?" I asked.

"Yeah," said Pops, "you need to know to be gentle. I love you, kiddo, but you can barge into a story, no holds barred. This time, you need to listen. Listen not only to her but to the Holy Spirit too. Listen when He says to pause, and wait on His timing. Ask fewer questions, and let the woman talk."

I wrote *LISTEN* in my notebook and underlined it. "Thanks, Pops! Love you!" I said as I hung up the phone.

On the drive to Molly's house, I began to rehearse questions in my head. The trees passed by as I made my way closer to the edge of town. Smythville was a relatively small town, but even small towns have dangerous areas. I silently prayed as I drove, asking God for protection and favor. My eyes drifted to the glove compartment, where I kept my handgun. I shook my head and kept driving, finally pulling into Molly's driveway.

Her house was more like a trailer that someone had tried to turn into a house. It had rickety steps leading up to a torn screen door. The inside door was open, and I could hear a trashy reality show playing at full volume. I subconsciously rolled my eyes. Who cared about which sister was dating whom?

I triple-checked the lock on my car and walked up to the trailer. I knocked on the edge of the doorframe. "*Molly?*" I yelled through the screen.

No response. I tried again, even louder. Still no response. I decided to poke around and walked to the backyard.

There was an old picnic table behind the house. A woman in leggings and a ratty tank top sat on it, smoking a cigarette and looking out at the trees that lined the clearing. She had a cell phone and a shotgun sitting next to her, so I cleared my throat from far off.

"Molly?" I called softly this time.

She whipped her head around and grabbed the gun. I noticed that she moved stiffly and that a large bandage covered her right shoulder and chest.

I held up my hands, showing her my notepad and pen. "My name is Julie! I'm an investigative reporter, and I just want to talk to you."

"How did you find me?" she demanded.

I slowly began to lower my hands as I stared into the barrel of the gun. "I've been investigating the POTG for months now.

No one ever talks about what they do, but I heard you wanted to talk to someone . . ."

Molly was visibly shaking, her finger hovering over the trigger. "There's a reason no one talks! Do you think they're just friendly neighborhood vigilantes?"

"Vigilantes?" I asked, confused.

"Yes, vigilantes. Do you know what they did to me?" she asked, her voice trembling as she jumped up and started pacing. Then she stopped abruptly and lowered the gun, letting the tip rest in the grass. "They stapled their calling card to my chest! Like a red letter. And that was nothing compared to the other things they did . . ."

I slowly began walking toward her. She was frozen, looking a mile away. I grabbed the gun from her left hand and laid it down on the grass.

"Molly," I said, laying my hand on her left shoulder, "what happened to you?"

She shifted her gaze to me. Her eyes were hollow. I could tell that her pain went deeper than just the events of last week. This woman was carrying years of pain.

"Please," I said, "I just want to know the truth. I won't use your name; I just want to bring this group to justice."

She shrugged off my hand and walked back to the table. Gingerly, she sat down, wincing at the pain. She pulled another cigarette out of the pack and lit it with shaky hands. "What the heck," she said, "let's get these scumbags!"

I sat down across from her and pulled out my phone. "Is it okay if I record this?" I asked.

She nodded and took a long drag of her cigarette. I started a new recording on my app and introduced Molly. "Is there an alias you want to go by?" I asked.

"Linda."

"Alright, Linda, how did you get the wound on your chest?"

She wouldn't look at me, but she faced the phone. "A couple of days ago, I was working my normal alley."

She looked at me, and I nodded. We both knew what she had been doing.

"A man pulled up and asked if I wanted to grab a bite at the bar. I was flat broke, not a penny to my name, and I had no dates that night, so I agreed. I jumped in his car, and he started driving. He was quiet. He seemed almost nervous. We drove by the bar and kept going, and I got scared. But I figured maybe he was from out of town, so he didn't know his way around, ya know?"

I nodded. "Can you describe this man?"

"He was just a man—tall, blond, nothing special. But when I asked him about turning back toward the bar, he ignored me, and he reached to grab my knee. I began to struggle, and he tightened his grip. When he pulled into a clearing, I started panicking."

She looked up at me and looked back down at her half-gone cigarette. "I was a little stoned when he asked me to come with him, but the sight of a bunch of people in black robes and masks where he stopped sobered me up right away. When I looked back at him, he had put on a black mask too and was holding up a gun. He told me to get out, so I did."

She paused and put her hands flat on the table. A million questions formed in my mind, but I silenced them, remembering what my grandfather had said. I paused and waited.

Molly looked me in the eyes. "Ya know, my life hasn't always been easy! I've had to fight for every scrap of food, every dollar. Some of us can't just walk around with our notebooks; we do what we can to survive."

She was angry, but I could tell she was ashamed too. I paused the recording.

"Molly, I'm not here to judge you." I tried to reassure her. "I'm here to learn the truth and to share your story. You can tell me as much or as little as you want, but don't hold back on my account."

She stared at me for another minute and then nodded at the phone. I started the recording again as she picked up her story.

"The driver told me to get into the center of the circle, and they closed in around me. Everywhere I turned, there was one of them, cutting off my exit. There was one man who had white sleeves on his black robe, and he spoke." She shuddered. "What he said, his voice, haunts every dream, every quiet moment. I can't escape him."

"What did he say?" I asked.

"He pointed his finger at me and said, 'Molly, we're the POTG. We seek to cleanse. We have found you guilty!' Then the group all chanted, 'We have found you guilty!' The driver pushed me to the ground and held his gun against my head. I was crying, but the leader kept going: 'You're dirty and ugly, and you shall not spread your disease! Your lifestyle must be exterminated.

You must be punished.' I remember being hit on the head and feeling a sharp pain, and then nothing."

I had read the officer's notes that were in her file. The men had drugged her, presumably to keep her out cold. Then they had brutally attacked her, cutting her so that she would never be able to have sex without pain again. She had almost died from the blood loss.

Molly lit another cigarette. As if remembering her manners, she offered me one, which I refused with a polite shake.

"When I woke up in the ER, the first thing I remember was seeing a nurse bending down to touch my chest. I shoved her, trying to get away, but an orderly came in and tied me down. It turns out that the men had stapled a note to my breast." She laughed dryly. "It said *Compliments of the POTG*, as if I were a present they were giving the police."

I had seen this note. It was nothing crazy, just a printed note, no recoverable DNA on it, besides her blood.

"Did the police interview you at the hospital?" I asked.

She nodded, "Yeah, but they did *nothing*. Apparently, I wasn't the first 'present' delivered to them. The POTG have been working this town for months." She shook her head. "Do you know what POTG stands for? *Punishers Of The Guilty*. Who are they to say that *I'm* the one who deserves to be punished? They're the cowards who are attacking defenseless women!"

I wrote "Punishers Of The Guilty" in my notebook and circled it.

"What are you going to do now?" I asked.

She flicked her cigarette ash to the ground. "I don't know. I might move out of state, ya know, get out of dodge. Maybe I'll start over somewhere else."

"Do you want to move?"

Her eyes got sad. "No, this is my home. But it's not safe for me anymore."

I nodded, and we both fell silent. I stopped the recording, and we just sat there as the shadows grew longer and longer. My heart was breaking for this woman. I had been raised Christian, but I had stopped going to church about a year ago. Yet I still talked to God all the time. As we sat, I threw all the questions I had wanted to ask her at God: *Why did this happen? What's going to happen to Molly now? I don't believe she deserved this, so why are You allowing it, God?*

The light of Molly's cigarette butt dimmed as she put it out on the wooden table. "Are we done?" she asked all of a sudden, getting up.

"We are," I said. I reached out and laid my hand on hers. "Thank you for sharing."

She flipped her dirty hair over her shoulder, and I saw the bruises on her collarbone. "The best thank-you would be finding out who these people are."

"Here," I said, writing my phone number down and sliding it over to her. "Call me or text me anytime. I'll let you know when the police get them."

I put my phone in my pocket and began to walk to my car.

"Hey!" Molly yelled.

I turned around and looked at her.

"Be careful!"

I nodded and watched as she picked up the shotgun and lit another cigarette. I got into my car and put my hands on the wheel, breathing deeply. If I had had any doubts before, they were gone now. I had to bring this group to justice.

A ding on my phone announced a new text. Molly had texted me a name: *Jerome*. Who was Jerome?

chapter two

The Victim

"A man was going down from Jerusalem to Jericho,
and he encountered robbers, and they stripped him and
beat him, and went away leaving him half dead."

LUKE 10:30 NASB

The next day, I called the police station, asking about a "Jerome." But Dave, my contact, didn't have anything on him. I was confused, so I drove over to speak with Dave in person. I pulled up to the station and saw a hot pink Lexus parked outside. I rolled my eyes. What an annoying vehicle.

When I walked in, the receptionist stopped me. "Julie?" she asked.

"Yes?" I responded. "I'm here to meet with . . ."

"Me!" a bright voice called out from down the hall. I heard the click of stilettos and saw a woman walking toward me. She didn't belong in a police station, that was for sure. She was a tiny blonde woman who wore a dress of the brightest pink I had ever seen. She had a purse on her arm that cost as much as my car and enough sparkly jewelry to blind me. She held out her hand.

"Hello, Julie! I'm Frances! I'm so glad we finally get to meet!"

Finally? I thought. *This woman, Frances, must have the wrong girl.* Her smile never left her face, and I found myself reaching for my sunglasses.

"I'm the new Public Relations Representative for the Smythville Police Department. I've heard a lot about you!"

I heard the threat in her voice and smiled at her. "That's weird! Because I've never heard of you!" I shot back, mocking her perky energy.

She giggled, and I winced. "I'm on assignment from the state government," she told me. "Your city has a teeny bit of a confidentiality problem! From now on, if you want information, you can come to me."

My heart sank. *This is my new contact?* I groaned inwardly. *There go my leads! This ditz isn't going to give me any information.*

My smile fell, and hers ramped up another ten degrees. "Let me know if you need anything," she added. "I took the liberty of pulling the file on Jerome for you."

Frances pulled a hot pink file out of her purse and handed it to me. I gingerly opened it up. It was empty.

"Are you serious?" I asked her.

"Unfortunately, yes. This is all the information we are free to release to civilians at the moment." She looked at me almost apologetically before her fake smile returned.

"What about the Freedom of Information Act?" I asked, exasperated. "What about public safety?"

She placed her hand on my shoulder and looked me in the eyes. "Members of the public are as safe as they can be. I trust our fine detectives to do their jobs."

I handed her back the file and left. I was done with this woman; it was time to find another source.

I called Molly when I got back in the car, but the call went to voicemail. I texted her and asked where I could find Jerome. I could see that she read my message, but she didn't respond. I punched my steering wheel, frustrated. What was I going to do?

Like manna from heaven, the echoes of an ambulance sounded, and the thought hit me: *I need to go to the hospital and talk to Mary, the nurse!* Surely, she would help me. I zoomed down the road, following the ambulance, and arrived at the hospital in record time. I ran up the stairs and found Mary in the room of the first POTG victim I had seen, taking his vitals.

"Mary?" I asked.

She turned to me and held up her finger as she watched the seconds and counted his heartbeats.

"Isn't there a machine that does that?" I asked.

"Yes," she said, "but I like the physical touch that this offers me." The patient was still in restraints, which I thought was a good thing for her in that case.

She wrote down the man's heart rate and walked me out of the room. "How can I help you?"

I whispered, "Do you know a victim named Jerome?"

She looked up and down the hallway, and nodded. "Jerome Gorinski. He's in the rehab clinic, room 1030."

I was surprised, but I jotted down his name and room number. "Thank you so much! Can I ask why you're helping me?"

She sighed and leaned back against the wall. "I'm tired. This gang has hurt so many people in so many ways, and I'm tired of only being able to help their victims after the attacks."

I squeezed Mary's hand and set off down the hall. I didn't know if the police were sending anyone to stop Jerome from talking to me, but if they were, I needed to beat them there. As I attempted to find his room, I searched "Jerome Gorinski" on my phone. It turned out that this victim was a famous MMA (Mixed Martial Arts) fighter. The pictures of him all showed a huge guy who looked as if he could take just about anyone in a fight. He had given earlier interviews about his childhood, citing his abusive older brother as his reason for getting into fighting in the first place. He famously claimed, "I'm a born fighter, and my combat instincts are deadly." He had an impressive 12-2 record, and before he had his "accident," he was poised to take his next fight by a landslide.

I didn't find any information on Jerome's mishap, except for an interview with the local pastor who had spied his body on the side of the road but who hadn't stopped to help. The church's spin was that Jerome had been attacked, but that this pastor had good reasons why he had been unable to stop at the time. So he had prayed for someone else to find the man, and someone did. That sounded wrong, and as I finally found room 1030 in the rehab clinic, I had about a dozen questions prepped in my mind. Nothing prepared me for what I found.

Jerome lay on the bed, holding his right hand in front of his face and bending his fingers in and out. I knocked lightly, and he looked up at me. He had bandages wrapped around his head and arms, and his left hand was completely bandaged. At first glance, I thought he wore a white shirt, but he was shirtless, with what looked like a mile of bandages covering his chest. The ones on the left side of his chest were soaked in some sort of balm that made the room smell like an herb garden.

"Are you Julie?" he asked.

"Yes. Are you Jerome?"

"I am. Please, come sit down." He waved at the easy chair next to the bed.

I moved a stack of sheets out of the way and sat down next to him. I was a little surprised at his familiarity with me. "How do you know my name?"

He tapped his phone. "Molly told me you would come. We were neighbors upstairs, you know."

I didn't know, but I nodded. "Can I ask you some questions?" I asked.

"You can," he answered. "But if you like, I can tell my story and you can break in if you need to. You can record it if you like."

I nodded and put my phone on the tray table in front of him. He was friendly and open, not at all what I expected. He reached for the remote and moved his hospital bed into a sitting position.

I paused and thought about Pop's advice. "Are you okay with sharing all this information?" I asked. "I don't want to overwhelm you."

"That's okay. I need to tell someone everything," he answered. "The one thing I ask is that you don't write while I'm talking." He reached out with a bandaged hand and pushed my notebook down. "Look at me like I'm a person, please?"

I nodded and closed my notebook. That was a little hard for me since I was such a habitual notetaker, but I really didn't need notes anyway since I was recording the interview.

"You know about my past, yeah?"

I nodded.

"Alright, so you know that I'm a born fighter, and that my combat instincts are deadly."

I smiled at his tagline, and he smiled back at me.

"To be honest, I'm really proud of my fighting abilities, and I've always been able to defend myself. I'm not a little boy getting beat up at home anymore. I can take care of myself. But what happened to me was the craziest thing that I've ever experienced. If I were hearing the story, I would be like, *Nah, man, there's no way*. But this happened—to me! Of all people, this happened to me!"

Jerome took a breath, and I could feel his rage building. He unclenched his right fist, and I could see the scabs from the superficial wounds.

"When did the attack happen?" I prompted.

"It was a month and a half ago. I was walking down the county road to my friend's cabin. I like to walk along Route 8.

It's peaceful. But that night, a van slammed to a stop in front of me. I jumped back, mad as heck."

He went on: "The side door flew open, and a group of, like, five dudes jumped out. And one of them was actually a woman! They looked as if they were on their way to, like, a comic show or something. They all had the weirdest weapons."

I tilted my head, confused. "What do you mean?"

"Well, one guy had nunchucks and was, like, whipping them around. There was also one chick who had a police baton, and she was hitting her palm with it. I can't remember them all, but one other dude had one of those old-fashioned tonfas, like Sherlock Holmes used to carry. They looked kind of stupid, you know? All these little wimpy dudes and a girl standing in front of a professional fighter, and I almost laughed. Then the driver got out and walked over to the group. He was sliding his brass knuckles onto his hands, and that's when I started to get nervous. This dude was about my height, and if he got the drop on me first, I didn't know what I would do."

"What did he look like?" I probed for details.

"He was tall, had spiky brown hair and this crazy look in his eyes. He looked hungry and angry and excited all at the same time. It was freaking weird. The wimps all moved to let him stand in front of me, and he stepped up. I dropped my backpack and met his gaze. He asked me what my name was, where I was going, and who I thought I was—you know, typical fight stuff."

"What did you say?" I asked, leaning forward.

"Nothing, I just let him run his stupid mouth. While he talked, he started getting ramped up, and the next thing I knew, he was screaming at me. His buddies surrounded me, so I couldn't just walk away. I knew I'd have to fight these guys, so I started making plans. I needed to take out the followers first, and then I could take the leader. While I was keeping an eye on the guys and trying to decide which of them to tackle first, the girl with the police baton made the first move. I wasn't expecting that. She whacked my shins, and I fell to my knees. The leader goes, 'On your knees, where you should be! For I am Jupiter, and you will always bow before me!' Like some sort of freaking cult leader. I moved forward to grab him by the legs, but he punched me in the jaw, knocking out some of my teeth. Then he told me to get up and take off my clothes."

"What?!" I asked. "Why?"

"Dude, I have no idea, but some of those little idiots looked as though they wanted to see what was underneath, and I didn't want to show them. Jupiter grabbed my hair and yelled in my face, '*Take them off!*' So I did."

Jerome paused, swallowing, and he looked down at his bandaged left hand, which lay on the table.

"I left my boxer shorts on, but, you know, they just kept looking . . ."

As I was listening, my blood turned to ice. This man was broken, ashamed, and I doubt he had told anyone this part of the story. *This guy, Jupiter, is a sick, sick man*, I thought. I paused and let Jerome be quiet a minute.

Then he looked up at me. "They didn't, you know, *do* anything to me in *that* way. But I was just . . . there."

"You don't have to explain. What happened was sick and wrong."

He nodded and asked me to get him some water. I brought him a cup.

Jerome took a drink, steadied himself, and then continued his story: "After I took off my clothes, they kicked my backpack and clothes around and started jeering at me. I had reached the end of my patience, so I lunged at the guy with the nunchucks, you know, because that's such a stupid weapon. But this jerk had clearly used them before, and he flicked one of them at my face. It hit me square in the eye, and I immediately saw blood."

He lifted up part of the bandage around his head and showed me a jagged cut that was dangerously close to his eye.

"The doctor said if it had been any closer, I would have lost my eye," he went on. "But after that hit, I couldn't see, and they all basically started beating on me. I was swinging punches, sometimes hitting, but mostly missing. It was as if this group had done this before, because each one would hit me or attack me, and then yell out, '*Your turn!*' to one of the others. And the next one would step in. Freaking Jupiter just watched it go down, laughing and cleaning his nails with a knife. I finally grabbed onto one of them and got him in a sleeper hold, but then it all came crashing down. All of them started attacking me at once. Finally, the old-timey baton guy hit my head. I let his buddy go and fell on the ground. Jupiter walked over and reached down to cut off my boxers. He leaned in and whispered, 'I want my face to be the last thing you remember.' I remember asking him why he was doing this, and he laughed and said, 'Because I can.' He stomped on my left hand, shattering all the bones, and I screamed. He took his knife and carved up my chest while some of his wimps held me down, and then he hit me in the head. I passed out."

I was horrified. My stomach reeled, and I felt frozen with fear and disgust. "What did he carve on your chest?" I asked, a guess already at the forefront of my mind.

"He carved *POTG*. The name of their stupid little club. The same group who messed with Molly, you know?"

Jerome hit the desk and knocked my phone off. "It just makes me *soooo* mad! They run around doing whatever they want, but no one will stop them. I didn't even do anything!"

I picked up my phone and paused the recording. This was way more than I had ever thought. The story I was chasing, of the dark club who sought to enact their own form of justice, was disappearing. Jerome hadn't done anything criminal, like the other POTG victims. He was innocent. They had attacked him just for fun.

"What happened next?" I asked after a minute, starting the recording again.

"Well, like I said, I passed out, but can I tell you what the police told me?"

I nodded.

"So apparently, I was lying by the side of the road for a while. A pastor drove by and saw me, but he was in a rush or something, so he didn't stop."

"Yeah," I interrupted, "have you spoken with him?"

"No," said Jerome, "but he came into the hospital and told everyone that he had prayed for someone to save me and his prayer had been answered, because someone did. He got his picture taken with me after one of my surgeries, while I was still under."

I wrinkled my nose. That was a disgusting bit of PR posturing. That was also one of the reasons I hadn't been to church. The pastor, Pastor Liam, wasn't my favorite person, and to hear that he was benefiting from this story enraged me. I felt the Holy Spirit gently check my spirit, however, and my storm of anger subsided a little.

Jerome nodded. "My thoughts exactly. I remember waking up on the side of the road when another man saw me and pulled over. I remember him pouring disinfectant on my chest and forcing pain pills down my throat. He wrapped me up in a blanket and then, like, somehow put me in the bed of his truck. I blacked out again, but I remember pain-filled glimpses of that night. I now know that this other guy took me to the nearest hotel and loaded me onto one of those luggage cart things, you know? Then he and the hotel clerk put me in a bed and started taking care of me. I remember an older lady giving me water. The guy was putting ointment on my cuts. I know he relocated my shoulder and cleaned out the gash by my eye."

"Why didn't they call the hospital?" I asked.

"So, this guy—his name is Harvey—has first-aid and triage experience. He knew he could get me stable, and the hospital was too far away. Lydia, the older lady, told me that they did call 911, but that because of the distance and another emergency situation going down, an ambulance couldn't make it until morning. Harvey stayed by my bedside and helped control the bleeding, and when I woke up in the morning, he was gone. Then the ambulance arrived and took me to the hospital, and Lydia came along for the ride."

My fingers itched for my notebook, but I kept repeating in my head, *Harvey, Harvey, I have to find out who this Harvey is.* "Did Harvey ever come to visit you?"

"No, but I am kind of surprised that he stopped to help me that night at all."

"Why?"

"Well, I'm a pretty basic dude, you know? But according to Lydia, this guy Harvey was . . . different."

"Different how?"

Jerome rubbed the back of his neck. "Well, Lydia told me that he had a gay pride sticker on his truck and that he had to pay her in cash because he didn't have legal documentation to be in the country."

I was confused. In my quick Internet searches of Jerome, I had seen multiple articles where he was pretty outspoken against many things, including illegal immigration, abortion, gay rights, and what he once called "the greatest scam of the century," or global warming. By all accounts, Jerome was a fairly famous conservative guy. It had gotten him in trouble in the past, and he was well known for seeking out arguments. In fact, he was actively involved in political circles, where he was looking to make legal changes. If this Harvey guy knew who Jerome was and what he believed, that would be . . . astounding that he stopped to help him. Who would go out of their way to save someone who was so fiercely against them and their culture?

Jerome seemed embarrassed. "I'm not saying I agree with everything this guy stands for, but I do know I would've definitely died if he hadn't stopped to help. So, you know . . ."

He leaned into the phone, "Harvey, if you're reading this in the newspaper, man, let's get lunch sometime, bro. Let me thank you."

I chuckled and stopped the recording. I sat and talked with Jerome for a little while longer. He was a nice guy, and although he seemed like a pretty stereotypical "man's man," he had a lot to say. When the rehab nurse came in to change his bandages, he asked if I wanted to see what the gang had done to him, and I agreed to stay. I had already seen a lot of what the POTG club had done, but this was the most gruesome and egotistical example of cruelty I had ever seen. The scarring was horrific, and the letters were grotesquely legible. I swallowed hard and tried to maintain my composure. He looked at me and offered a crooked smile.

"Are you going to get a skin graft?" I asked.

"I don't know yet," Jerome replied. "I'd like to, but also, I don't want this club to know that they got to me, you know? They tried to kill me, but I'm still here."

"Why do you think they did what they did?" I questioned.

"I don't know. Honestly, I think they're a bunch of cowards who can't fight a man face-to-face. The whole group of them are, like, forgettable. Except that Jupiter. Man, he is a cruel, cruel dude. What kind of person looks someone in the eyes and then does what he did? He's a psycho, I can tell you that much!"

I thanked Jerome and promised to look into finding Harvey. I wanted to find this "hero" and hear his side of the story. But I also wanted to take the POTG club down. And I wanted to hear Pastor Liam's side of the story. As much as I disliked Pastor Liam, he had played a role in this story. Hearing Jerome's side of it had put me ill at ease. *Maybe Pastor Liam thought he saw another car slowing down to help,* I thought, trying hard to give him the benefit of the doubt. *Or maybe he could give me some other insight into why he didn't stop.* At the very least, a trip to church would give me the opportunity to pray in a pew again (something I secretly missed, but only in times of real crisis lately). It was time to go to church.

chapter three

The Priest

"And by chance a priest was going down on that road,
and when he saw him, he passed by on the other side."
LUKE 10:31 NASB

I pulled up to Fellowship Church and shifted my car into park. Historically, I had not had positive experiences at this church. Pastor Liam, the senior pastor, was a good preacher, but he and his wife could be extreme in their convictions. I remember a few months ago when my aunt had sold her first book of poetry, they had told the church members to burn the book because she used a swear word in one of the poems. But a good reporter can put her emotions on hold for the story, right?

I said a quick prayer and got ready to walk in. It was a Wednesday night, so Pastor Liam was wrapping up his midweek service. A small part of me was glad to see only a few cars in the parking lot. I brushed the metaphorical chip off my shoulder and walked in. The congregation was gathered in the lobby area, exchanging opinions on the sermon and gossiping. I saw Miss Carol, a beautiful older woman whom I had known my whole life. She came up and gave me a hug. I couldn't help but smile as I hugged her back.

"Miss Carol, is Pastor Liam here?"

"Yes, honey, he's in the sanctuary. Head right on in."

I smiled and gave her another hug. Then I walked into the sanctuary and felt the rush of cool air on my skin. The lights were still on, but the sound system had been shut down. Pastor Liam sat in the front row, writing notes in his journal. I approached him and reached out to tap his shoulder.

"Pastor Liam?" I asked softly, but firmly.

He looked up, and recognition dawned in his eyes. "Good evening, Julie," he said. "I've been expecting you for some time now."

A burst of anger hit me. If he had been expecting me, why hadn't he reached out? I swallowed and asked if I could sit down and ask him some questions as a reporter.

"Yes, but please record the whole conversation. You can never be too careful."

I silently agreed and started the recording on my phone.

"Can you state your name and occupation for the record, please?"

"My name is Pastor Liam Fredrick, and I'm a minister of the Gospel of Jesus Christ at Fellowship Church, right here in Smythville."

I was taking down notes, and he waited for me to finish before asking, "What exactly would you like to know?"

"Well," I responded, "as you know, I'm working on a story for *The Journal* on the POTG attacks." He nodded as I continued: "Almost two months ago, a young man was brutally beaten by the club and was left for dead. By your own account, on the night of the attack, you drove by this man and saw him, but you left him by the side of the road. Can you tell me why?"

Pastor Liam leaned back and rested his arm on the pew, adjusting his suit jacket. "Certainly. Are you familiar with the calling that God has for pastors?"

I nodded. "I was raised in church, but I'd like to hear about your experience with it."

"Alright," he started. "To understand this calling, you must understand me, my dear. I'm a simple man, raised by a farmer and a godly woman. I was called into the ministry at a young age. I remember sitting at the kitchen table with my mother and telling her that God was calling me. She took my hands and placed them on her Bible, and we prayed together."

His eyes wandered off, tears beginning to form. "My mother was my favorite person, and the lessons she taught me made me the man I am today."

Pastor Liam got quiet, and I sat with him in respectful silence. He cleared his throat and began again: "One of the most important lessons my mother taught me was always to go back to the Bible for everything. I base my opinions, my actions and my beliefs on this book right here." He held up his Bible and then opened it. "I began to follow the Bible's teachings from an early age. In school, I was extremely careful about whom I was friends with. First Corinthians 15:33 says, *'Bad company corrupts good character.'* My mother tried her best to pray a hedge of protection over me, but my school was still full of many pitfalls. I've always been introverted, so when guys at school would pick on me for being quiet, I would let it roll off my back, because only the Bible can tell me who I am. When I was a freshman in high school, a young man transferred into our class. Right away, I didn't trust him. I could tell something was off about him, and I was right. He was a homosexual. But I knew that God was teaching me a lesson. My mother and I began to pray for this young man, but I knew better than to be his friend. I would not allow myself to be corrupted by his company."

Pastor Liam looked as though he was about to launch into a tirade, so I quickly broke in. "What did you do for your university experience after high school?"

He smiled and pulled out his phone, showing me his screen-saver. The image was of him standing with his wife in front of a tower made of bricks and glass.

"This is my wife and me in front of my alma mater, Ashburn Bible School. We met there and got married our senior year of our undergrad studies. I went on to get my Master of Divinity degree before deciding to go home and pastor the local church. From there, God has called us to different churches in different seasons, and He has us here in Smythville for right now."

Here he paused and picked up his Bible again. "I'm not a perfect pastor, but I am who I am. I have always been a reserved and quiet man, so it would make sense that the way I pastor reflects my personality. It's not my job to fix everyone's problems. It's my job to be who I am; it's God's job to fix people. If they need counseling, they go to a counselor. If they need doctoring, they go to a doctor. If they need theological advice and guidance, they come to me."

"But what about all the stories where Jesus came across broken people and healed them?" I asked.

He laughed. "He was *Jesus*! I'm just Liam. At the end of the day, judgment and vengeance belong to the Lord. I'm here to teach. Jesus was probably an extrovert, which is why He was so good with people. I'm not always good with people, so I stay in my lane."

"So," I asked, "in reference to the events of that night . . ."

"Yes, well, I was on my way to my weekly Bible study. I was running late. When I saw the man, of course I felt deep compassion. But realistically, how much good could I have done for him? I'm not a doctor; I'm not a first responder. I'm a theologian."

"I thought you were a pastor?" I broke in.

"I'm both," he responded, slightly flustered. "I'm a pastor by job and a theologian by choice."

"Let me make sure I understand this clearly," I began. "You call yourself a pastor, but when you see someone lying on the ground, beaten almost to death, you keep driving because of your theological convictions."

"You're making me sound like a monster!" he cried. "I'm just a man! I did what I could. I prayed that God would send another person to save him—*and He did*. I simply did exactly what someone in my position should have done in that moment. Besides, how was I supposed to know the guy was innocent? He could have been a member of the POTG club who had failed to do what they wanted, or he could have been a vagrant who had attacked some innocent person."

"But," I countered, "the POTG has been committing these crimes for months in this area. Didn't you think that the man lying there might have been the victim of one of these attacks?"

"It occurred to me. But how was I to know that the man was still alive? Or how was I to know that he didn't deserve what happened to him? The POTG club has been targeting some pretty nasty characters. What if the guy had received what he deserved?"

My patience almost broke at that point. "What do you mean, *what he deserved?*" I asked in a quiet, controlled voice.

"You know—the justice of God is shown in different ways through Scripture. Look at Sodom and Gomorrah."

"What about the woman at the well?" I countered, heart hammering in my chest.

"That's what I'm saying," Pastor Liam continued. "We don't know why God does things the way He does. We just have to trust in Him and do what He has called us to do."

A storm of rage began building in me. *How DARE he?* I thought. *This is the man who is supposed to be the moral standard in this town, and he's arguing for the actions of this horrific club?!*

I think Pastor Liam could sense my anger. He reached his hand out to pat my knee. "Have faith, Julie. God is in control."

Golly, I hoped so. Pastor Liam needed to receive what was coming to *him*. I'd heard it said that pastors who don't smell like sheep have no place in leadership, and I 100 percent agreed. His "theology," and the way he rationalized his actions based on it, made me sick. I felt the Holy Spirit check me again, but I was confused. I felt Pastor Liam was everything that a pastor should *not* be. I felt I had every right to be angry at this man!

I had learned from Pops that practicing my professionalism meant controlling my tongue in situations, like this, that pushed my buttons, so I bit back the sarcastic reply in my head, calmly thanked Pastor Liam for his time, and ended our interview. As I walked out the doors of the sanctuary, I looked back and saw him reading his Bible. Almost all the lights were off, and the full moon illuminated him. In that moment, I felt sorry for him. He knew the Scriptures so well, and he thought he knew what they meant. Yet he had no idea what it meant to love people the way they deserved to be loved. Or to extend mercy to them that they might not deserve, as Jesus did every day of His life on earth.

Pastor Liam was stuck in the world of his own mind. Learning to take risks and love people with his actions was a joy he had yet to experience. He was missing out on so much because he never looked for God anywhere outside the Bible. My aunt used to read me the Psalms whenever we hiked, and I have memories of learning how creation declared the glory of God, while we looked out at snowcapped mountain peaks. I'm not sure Pastor Liam ever related the revelation he was reading in God's Word to the realities of everyday life. I don't think he knew how, or he wouldn't have passed by a man like Jerome, who was bleeding and dying right in front of him.

The conversation I had with Pastor Liam offered me no information for my article, but it did clue me in to what he had been thinking that would make him pray for someone else to help Jerome instead of stopping himself to take action. Nothing he said excused him in my mind, but it sure explained some things! But for now, I had reached a dead end with Pastor Liam. Where would I go next?

chapter four

The Levite

"Likewise a Levite also, when he came to the place
and saw him, passed by on the other side."
LUKE 10:32 NASB

I was stuck. There was nothing I hated more than being backed into a corner with nowhere to go. Over the next three days, I listened again to my recorded interviews, typed up all my notes, and began to search for this "Harvey" guy everywhere, but to no avail. On the walls of my office were the news stories of my personal heroes: the "Spotlight" story from Chicago that exposed corruption in the Catholic Church, the *Times* article that introduced COVID-19 before it even left the city of Wuhan and even *The Washington Post* article that broke the Watergate scandal. All these reporters persevered through their setbacks. I spun around in my chair, trying to get the creative juices flowing. Journalism was 80 percent hard work and 20 percent luck, and I needed some good luck right about now.

I didn't want to cook, so I went to Mom's Table, the local diner. Smythville was a small town, so all the waitresses knew me and my order, and they smiled at me as I sat down in an empty booth. I pulled out my notebook and started to write down article title ideas. As I scribbled away, my thoughts drifted to Jerome. I hoped his wounds were healing well. He was so lucky that this Harvey guy had stopped to help him. I prayed, asking God to heal him, and also asking Him to direct me where to go next.

Then it hit me! I needed to find the hotel that Harvey had stopped at. Why hadn't it occurred to me before? I thanked God and started planning my drive. Behind me, I heard two women praying for their meal. I listened in to their prayer as the second woman ended her portion with, "And dear Lord, bless and keep Kara's sleep. Erase the memory of the bloody man she saw by the side of the road, and bring her peace." I snapped to attention and had to keep myself from whipping my head around to start asking questions.

The women continued with their meal as the waitress placed a plate with a Reuben and fries down in front of me. I smiled my thanks and began crunching on the extra pickles I had asked for, trying to formulate a game plan and continuing to eavesdrop on the two women. Whoever this woman, Kara, was, it sounded as if she had seen Jerome that night, and it was possible that she had seen Harvey, too.

Is this an answer to my prayer for direction already? I wondered. *Thank You, Lord!*

I needed to get this woman's story. Like another answer to prayer, one of the women finally left. I turned around and asked the other one how she had enjoyed her meal.

She looked up from her phone, slightly confused. "It was good . . ." she said warily.

"My name is Julie. I'm an investigative reporter. Do you mind if I ask you a few questions?"

"Questions? About what?"

I got up from my table and went to sit across from her. "I hope you don't mind, but I overheard the prayer about Kara, who saw a bloody man by the road. I think she may have seen the body of a victim named Jerome Gorinski before he was discovered and brought to the hospital. Are you Kara? I'm writing an article on the POTG club, and I want to find out everything I can about this story."

She sighed and nodded. This woman, Kara, was very young, younger than I was. She looked to be in her early twenties, and she was dressed stylishly. There were a Bible and a journal sitting in front of her, and she nervously tapped her pen on the journal's cover.

Suddenly, Kara looked down at her smartwatch and smacked her hand to turn off the screen. "I would love to help you, but I'm running late for my small group. I'm so sorry!"

"That's okay!" I said quickly. "Let me get your phone number, and we can schedule a time to meet up."

She paused, and I could tell that she genuinely wanted to help. Or she just wanted to be interviewed. Either way, she handed me her phone, and I put in my number and name. She texted me her number, and I promised to follow up.

"I don't know how I can help you, but I'll do what I can," Kara said, grabbing her bag and slinging it over her shoulder. "Right now, I have to leave!"

I thanked her again and sat back in my booth. I typed out a quick text, asking her if we could meet tomorrow or the next day, and then I started a to-do list. I needed to interview Kara, find the hotel, and find out who Harvey was. Maybe Frances, the SPD's new PR lady, could help me. I laughed to myself at that thought. That woman was going to be absolutely no help. But as I thought about who could help me, my phone rang. It was my editor, Mark.

"Julie!" he started, as soon as I answered the phone, "I need that story!"

"I know, Mark," I said, "but I need another extension." I figured I needed another month to find Harvey and type up his story. I still didn't know where this story was going, and I needed a conclusion.

"No time, Buttercup," he said. "There's another victim who's talking to the *Gazette*."

I pulled my phone away from my ear and put my forehead on the table in front of me. The *Smythville Gazette*? It was a trashy local paper, whose biggest story last year was the mayor's brother's divorce. *The Journal* had a larger audience, and our main offices were in the capital, about a three-hour drive from

Smythville. But in the time since the POTG attacks, the *Gazette* had become opportunist, reporting all the gory details its reporters could find. Thankfully, their team was almost as incompetent as I was hardworking, so I almost always got exclusive rights. But this time, they had beaten me. I had been so wrapped up in Jerome's story that I hadn't been trolling the hospital or the police scanners.

"Who's the victim?" I asked.

"She's just a kid—trailer trash, right? And apparently everyone knew she was a little thief."

I interrupted him to ask, "Is her name Grace?"

"Yeah, but don't interrupt me."

Grace was a legend among the local high schoolers. She was famous for stealing things and then displaying them publicly. Last year for homecoming, she stole a police car and put it in the middle of the local cemetery. When she was a little girl, her father taught her close-up magic before he left her mom and her. She had used her skills for evil, becoming quite the little pickpocket.

I met Grace when she tried to steal my notepad while I was interviewing her friend, who had been shaved bald by the POTG club. This friend, Scarlett, had won a beauty pageant by sleeping with one of the judges. The act would have been legal, except that she was fifteen. The POTG club had exacted their punishment on her and on the guy, eventually blinding him. Grace had seemed pretty numb to the situation, and when I caught her trying to grab my notebook, she laughed and skipped away.

Mark's voice shocked me out of my memories: "Apparently, they cut off this Grace's thumb and dropped her off outside the ER, with the finger in a plastic baggie."

My Reuben turned to rock in my stomach. I had heard so many stories about this club, but their creativity and cruelty were still appalling.

"That's awful," I said into my phone.

"Yeah, it is, and having her start talking to the *Gazette* means I need your story pronto! Have you found the leader of the club yet?" Mark asked.

"No, but I want to take the story in a different direction." I outlined what had happened to Jerome.

Mark was quiet as he thought. "Alright," he finally said, "find this Harvey guy, but also find that Jupiter character. He sounds like the leader. I want to know what he has to say, too. And Julie? Be careful! Make sure your contact at the SPD knows what kind of leads you're following to find the club's leader, just for safety's sake. I imagine they want to find him even more than you do!"

He hung up the phone, and I saw that Kara had texted me back, saying we could meet tomorrow morning in the park. I "liked" her message and then dropped a twenty on the booth behind me. I got up to leave and waved at the waitresses.

"Hey," one of them called out, "did you hear about Grace?"

I nodded, and she shook her head sympathetically. "Poor girl," the waitress sighed.

The next day, I grabbed a coffee and walked over to the park. Kara was sitting in the gazebo, writing in her journal, headphones in. I walked up the stairs, and she looked up and smiled at me, pulling her headphones out of her ears and putting them in the case.

"Good morning, Julie!" she said, getting up to shake my hand.

"Good morning!" I said. Apparently, we were both morning people, because she looked as awake as I was. "Do you mind if I record this interview?" I asked.

"Not at all," she said, pulling her hair up and securing it.

I started out with the typical questions, and I learned that she was 23 and worked from home for a nonprofit that built wells in Africa. She had grown up in the Smythville area and loved going to church. But when Pastor Liam and his wife took over Fellowship Church, she had not liked them. So she started attending a church in the next town over.

"How much time do you spend over there?" I asked.

"Oh, I go almost every night!" she said. "I volunteer in the children's ministry, I attend Bible study twice a week, and I host a small group for young women."

"You must be very busy," I said. "What were you doing the night of the attack on Jerome Gorinski?"

"Well," she started, "that night we had a volunteer meeting. We have them about once a quarter, and we talk through the vision of the church and get important updates from the senior pastor and stuff like that."

"Do you attend all these meetings?"

"Yes, there's a portion of the night where the older volunteers and the elders of the church get to pray for the younger generation, and vice versa. It's absolutely powerful, so I never miss a meeting."

She picked up her iced coffee and took a drink, rattling the ice in the cup. Listening to Kara's list of church activities, I did have to admit that I missed church. I was never without God; that much I knew. But there was something about the togetherness of being in church that I really missed.

"So, on that night of the attack, you were driving home from the meeting at your church?" I asked.

"Yes," she said, nodding her head. "I like to listen to worship music and pray on my drive. It helps calm me down and keeps me focused. But that night, while I was praying, I hit a pothole and got a flat tire. So I pulled over. I got out of my car to check on my tire, but then I saw the blood."

She shuddered and looked off into the distance. "There was so much blood on the ground, and it got on my shoes! I could tell there was something on the other side of my car, and when I peeked over to see what had happened, all I saw was a pool of blood and some dirty clothes. I got really scared, so I got back in my car right away and tried to call my boyfriend."

"You didn't call the cops?" I asked.

"No, at first I thought it was a deer. Then, when I saw the clothes, I thought someone was still over there. I didn't want to freak the person out or make myself an easy target as the next victim."

I was confused. "What do you mean by that?"

She looked ashamed. "Well, I was really scared. I've heard stories about the POTG club, and I really like to watch true crime shows, so I thought maybe there was an attacker waiting for me. I had just listened to a podcast about a guy who pretended to be hurt so he could kidnap young women. I didn't want to freak out whoever was over there on the side of the road, or worse, put myself in danger."

As I took notes on her story, I shook my head. This fascination with true crime was not healthy. I could imagine this girl, paralyzed with fear by the side of the road, thinking there was someone in the bushes waiting for her. What lay in the bushes that night was actually a man close to death. In her fear for her own safety, she had missed out on the real victim.

"What did you do next?"

"Well," she said, taking a deep breath. "I couldn't get any cell service and my phone was almost dead, but good thing my dad had taught me how to change a tire. I had to get out of my car and deal with the flat tire, so I did it as quietly and quickly as possible."

"Did you hear or see anything out of the ordinary?"

"Not while I was changing the tire. The whole time, I was praying under my breath. When I got back in my car to drive away, the headlights shifted, and I saw the body." She picked up the pen that was laying on her journal and started twisting the cap on and off, almost subconsciously. "The man looked like something out of a nightmare. His face was bleeding, there was a leg bone poking out of his shin, and he was all cut up. I mean, I can't even tell you all of it, because I couldn't even look at him. I almost threw up because his blood was everywhere."

In my interview with Jerome, he hadn't told me the part about someone breaking his leg. I assumed that after he had passed out, the club had probably gone back and beaten him again before leaving him for dead. I made a note of that in my notebook as Kara continued.

"I didn't know what to do! It was so scary. I thought about calling the cops, but my phone had died, and I didn't have a charger in my car. I couldn't get out of my car and help the guy, because what if it were a trap? What if he were already dead? I couldn't help a dead man! So I drove away. I figured it was better—and a lot safer—if I just didn't get involved. While I was driving, I started praying, and by the time I got back to my house, I felt much better. I knew that God was going to take care of the guy."

I kept taking notes as Kara wrapped up her story and took another drink of her coffee, draining it down.

"You mentioned before that you volunteer in the children's ministry at your church. Have you received any first-aid training?"

She nodded, and I continued: "Did you think about maybe using your training to help the man at all?"

Kara started tapping the pen against the table. "Not really, no. I was absolutely *terrified*, and I was thinking more about how I could get to safety as quickly as possible."

I nodded and asked if she had seen Jerome since.

"No, but I heard that he survived the attack," she replied. "I hope the police absolutely destroy that POTG club! I hate not feeling safe in my own town. If your story can help get rid of them, I'm glad to have helped you in any way that I could."

I silently agreed with her about Smythville's streets starting to feel more and more dangerous. While I didn't agree that what she had done that night by driving away from Jerome's bleeding body was right, I could understand why the whole scenario had terrified her. I had noticed that as the attacks continued, I was feeling less and less safe in this town. I thought about the gun I had in my glove box and offered up a silent prayer that I would never have to use it.

"How are you doing with the memory of it all?" I asked.

She sighed. "Not well. I keep having nightmares, and my boyfriend and I broke up right after it happened, so this has been a rough couple of months for me."

I patted Kara's hand sympathetically, but inside I was thinking, YOU *had a rough couple of months?! Jerome almost died! And you were NO help at all!*

I had to remind myself that she was young and scared, and that considering her very sheltered life, she probably was having a rough time. But still, she should have at least called the police when she got home. Fear of getting involved, or worse, of getting hurt, makes people do crazy things.

I thanked Kara, and she asked if she could pray for me right there. I politely declined, but I asked her to include me in her daily prayers, and I told her she could pray that I would write a good story. She smiled and nodded, and then she took her headphones out of their case since our interview was over.

As I walked back to my car, I shook my head, thinking about Kara. She was a church kid, a sheltered girl who lived her life in a very clearly defined role. She lived, breathed, and was her church, and she served it pretty well. She knew how to be the church inside the four walls of her church, but outside the building, it was something else again. When it came down to it, her fear overshadowed everything, especially when it really counted.

I decided to go to the hospital and see if I could interview Grace, the latest victim. As I drove, I found myself pulling the gun out of the glove box and putting it in the center console of my car, in closer reach. This was no time for backing down from danger, and I needed to be prepared for anything.

chapter five

The Innkeeper

*"On the next day he took out two denarii and gave them
to the innkeeper and said, 'Take care of him; and whatever
more you spend, when I return, I will repay you.'"*
LUKE 10:35 NASB

As I drove back to the hospital, I passed the police station, where
Frances's pink car was parked. I shook my head and kept driving.
I had a victim to interview. As I drove, I started to pray aloud.
The times I spent with Jesus in my car always gave me perspec-
tive and helped me keep my heart from callusing. I told Him
about Jerome and everything that had happened. As I released
Jerome's story to Him, a huge weight lifted off my chest. I took
a deep breath and pulled into a parking spot.

On the recovery floor, I found there were police officers guarding the latest victim's door. When I tried to walk in, they shook their heads.

"Sorry, Julie," said Stan, the one on the left. "The victim doesn't want to talk to any more reporters."

I leveled my gaze at him. "Grace," I said. "Her name is Grace."

He smiled sheepishly, and I turned around and walked to the nurse's station. I wanted to say hi to Mary. When I asked the nurse on duty where Mary was, she told me to look for her outside in the garden, where she was eating lunch with her mother. I thanked her and headed out to say a quick hello.

When I reached them, I smiled as I saw a woman my age and her mother, both eating salads quietly. Mary put her head on her mom's shoulder, and her mom reached over to pat her cheek. Then Mary saw me and waved me over.

I smiled at her mom and then asked Mary, "How are you?" I gave her a quick hug and sat down with the two of them.

"I'm great! I get to have lunch with my mama, so today is a good day." She squeezed her mom, and her mom smacked her playfully.

"What are you up to, oh intrepid reporter?" Mary asked.

I laughed. "Well, I wanted to interview Grace, but now I'm off tracking down another lead, since the police are being so very kind and cooperative outside her room."

"Oooh," said her mother, laughing at my sarcasm, "which lead?"

"I'm looking for a woman named Lydia who works at a hotel just off the county road outside town. She was one of Jerome's saviors, and I want to hear her side of the story."

The two women exchanged a startled glance, an unspoken connection passing between them.

"Wait," I interjected, "are you Lydia?"

Mary's mom nodded. "I am Lydia. I assume you want to interview me?"

"Yes! If you don't mind, of course."

Mary nodded at her mother, and Lydia took a deep breath. "I'm glad to help."

As they finished their lunch, we chatted about our day. Lydia was well-spoken, and the bond she had with her daughter was evident. After the salads had been cleared away, I asked Lydia if I could record our interview, and she agreed, under the condition that I take her name off the record. I agreed to that and began the recording on my phone. I asked Lydia to state her name and age. She laughingly refused to give the latter, and then we started talking about her occupation.

"I've been a nurse my whole life. It must run in the family." She smiled at her daughter. "A couple of years ago I retired, but being a nurse is more like a calling than a job. So when I retired, I decided to keep taking care of people, but in a different way. My husband and I had always wanted to open a small hotel."

Here she paused, as tears began to well in her eyes. "Unfortunately, he died before we could make that dream happen together. But I decided to continue on. I bought a small roadside hotel and hired a team to fix it up for me."

"What's the name of your hotel?" I asked.

"The Samaritan," she said, laughing. "It was an old joke between my husband and me that he would take in anyone, even if the person was the dirtiest vagrant. He stopped and fed every homeless person and gave money to every charity. He was the kindest man I knew."

Mary nodded and gave her mom another hug, rubbing her arms. I gave Lydia a minute as she recovered.

"Do you remember a man named Harvey?" I asked.

"Yes," she said. "I remember the night I met him very well. Normally, I hire someone to work the night shift, but that night my employee called in sick. So I was sitting at the hotel desk instead. All of a sudden, I heard a truck come screeching into my parking lot. We didn't have any guests that night, or else the noise would have awoken them, for sure. A young man came running into the lobby and grabbed a luggage cart and ran out. I sensed something was amiss, so I followed him."

"What did the young man look like?" I asked.

"He was quite small, Latino, and he was wearing really short jean shorts and a pink shirt with a band name on it. His pink shirt was covered in red blood. I've seen a lot of gory things in my time, but what I saw in the back of his truck were some of the worst injuries I had ever seen on one person. I recognized the body at once. It was the young man who has been in the news a lot, Jerome something. He's the one trying to get those laws passed?"

I nodded, remembering the articles I had read about Jerome's penchant for all things politically conservative.

Lydia continued: "He had a broken leg, but there was a belt tourniquet on his thigh, and he was bleeding from lacerations on his head and chest. His arm hung out of the socket, and his chest was covered in fresh, deep cuts. When Harvey shone the light over him, I could see bruises beginning to develop on his sides, so I also thought that he had multiple broken ribs. His left hand was completely flattened, and Harvey had placed the hand across the man's abdomen. His nose was smashed in, and I could tell that Harvey had tried to bandage him up as best he could. There were scraps of blankets around his leg, and his arm was in a makeshift sling. I could smell liquor on the man's body, and I figured that Harvey had tried to sterilize the wounds."

I was writing down all the injuries as she listed them, and I asked, "What did Harvey say when he saw you had followed him outside?"

Lydia reflected for a minute. "He was in the truck bed, and he told me his name was Harvey. I asked if he had any medical training, and he said he did. We knew we needed to move the body inside, and he asked me if I thought I could carry the bottom half. I didn't think I could do it, but I knew that I'd just have to anyway. I grabbed Jerome's left leg and kept the board steady as Harvey gently pushed him out of the truck."

"Was Jerome wearing anything?"

"He was totally naked, but Harvey had wrapped a blanket around his middle. He had also laid him on a wooden board that had been in his truck, so we really just had to keep him stable and transfer the board to the luggage cart. I could see some bungee cords in the truck, so I assumed he had bound Jerome to the truck for the drive."

"Did anything about Harvey's actions stand out to you?" I asked.

"He was remarkably calm. He never yelled at me; he was very matter-of-fact about the instructions he gave. Oh, and he had one of those gay pride stickers on the rear window of his truck. Between that and his attire, I figured he was gay."

I paused and waited for her to continue. When she didn't, I prompted her, "Are there many gay people in these parts?"

"No," she said, "and to tell you the truth, I didn't really think about it until later, after we had taken Jerome to a room. We were able to get him onto the cart with minimal jarring, and I ran in to grab my nursing bag, which I still keep in case of emergencies. As Harvey wheeled him in, I directed him to the nearest room on the ground floor. It was a bit unwieldy to move Jerome, because Harvey had put the board lengthwise on the cart. The head and feet parts of the board were hanging over the sides, but we managed."

Lydia showed me what she meant with her hands, placing a fist under her open, flat palm. I nodded, and she continued: "When Harvey was able to get the cart into the room, we lifted Jerome onto the bed. Harvey slid the board out from under him and apologized to me for the blood on the sheets."

Lydia laughed and said, "I told him that it was no problem because I was used to it from being a nurse. Then I got to work seeing to Jerome's cuts. The worst was the head injury. I checked his pupils to see if they were blown, but miraculously, they were still intact. When Jerome was safely on the bed, Harvey asked if we had any alcohol. I pulled the rubbing alcohol out of my bag and told him to grab the bottles of whiskey that were under the front counter, a gift from a customer."

Lydia was certainly giving me the full story, and out of sheer habit I was scribbling down every detail she told me.

"When Harvey went to get the bottles, I started pulling out all my bandages and balms. I had some extra-strength painkillers that I normally use for my daughters' cramps. I managed to get those down his throat with a small amount of water. When Harvey came back, he told me he had already tried to sterilize some of the wounds with the tequila he had in his truck, but it hadn't been nearly enough. He poured the first bottle of whiskey from under the counter on the man's chest, head and leg, and the pain must have been overwhelming, because Jerome jerked awake and started screaming. We tried to hold him still as he screamed, and then finally he lost consciousness."

She kept going, "I ripped open my bandages and gave them to Harvey, who wrapped them around Jerome's head. I had no idea what to do with Jerome's smashed left hand, so I left it on his stomach and began to tend to his chest. I could tell that Harvey had already attempted to clean the lacerations out, but I tried to control the risk of infection. The cuts on his chest, which spelled out POTG, were horrific, but most of them were already beginning to clot. I washed them out with the second bottle of whiskey Harvey brought. Then I began to apply a salve I had made. I bandaged the wounds up to prevent infection. Harvey was busy, too. He grabbed Jerome's arm, reduced the shoulder back to its socket, and then placed Jerome's right hand across his stomach, taking care to avoid his mangled left hand. Harvey asked me to get some ice, so I went and grabbed a bag of ice and he put it on Jerome's shoulder."

It was clear that Lydia had extensive medical training. She delivered all these facts to me in the calmest tone, excluding nothing. Personally, all the details made me sick, and it was taking everything inside of me to keep listening. But it was my job. I swallowed down my revulsion and kept writing. Lydia paused and took a drink of her water, letting me catch up on my notes.

"Why didn't you call the hospital?" I asked.

"We did," she said. "I called the 911 dispatch and told them our location. My hotel is very far off the beaten track, and the hospital was going to receive a huge transfer of patients from two towns over. That location's power had gone out, and all the patients were being rushed to other hospitals. The closest hospital to me couldn't send an ambulance until the morning."

I shook my head. Poor Jerome! Nothing had gone right for him that night, except Harvey and apparently Lydia. "What happened after you stabilized Jerome?" I asked.

"Harvey and I went to the lobby, and I began to check Harvey in." Lydia giggled. "It seemed so ordinary compared to what we had just gone through. But when I asked him for his basic information, he couldn't give it to me. I remember that he put his arms on the counter and told me he was going to level with me."

She related what Harvey had disclosed to her. "'My visa isn't current,'" he told me, 'and I'm on my way to meet my boyfriend's family, so I need to pay you in cash for the room.'"

Lydia paused and looked slightly afraid. "I hadn't met very many gay people before, and I didn't really know what to say. I thought about calling the cops—because you know, he wasn't even in the country legally. Yet I found that I couldn't do it."

I nodded. "What did you do?"

"Well," said Lydia, "it's not as if I were going to turn out Jerome. And Harvey had been so kind and generous to both him and me. So I asked Harvey how long he wanted to book the room. He pulled out his wallet and paid me in cash for two nights, in advance. I thought this meant that he was going to stay on after Jerome had been admitted to the hospital, but as it turned out, the next morning Harvey left before the ambulance even came. He came to find me very early, thanked me, got in his truck and drove off. I guess he didn't want to be around, in case the police started asking any questions."

"Did Harvey leave any information on how to reach him?"

"Yes. When he was checking in, he gave me his email."

Lydia shared the email address with me and I wrote it down, underlined it, and circled it. "What did you do when the ambulance came?" I asked.

"The paramedics came in and started to transfer Jerome. They put in an IV and gave him a bolus of saline, trying to get his blood pressure under control. He had lost a lot of blood, so they called the hospital and prepared them. Then they loaded him up with morphine and moved him to a gurney. I asked them to take us to the Smythville Hospital, and I let my daughter know that we were coming."

Mary broke in, adding, "When Jerome arrived, I immediately asked to join his team and was granted special permission. I oversaw his nursing care from the moment he arrived until he was transferred to the rehab clinic."

"When you brought Jerome in, did anyone talk to you about what had happened?" I asked Lydia.

"Yes. I gave a statement to the police right after I arrived, but then no one came to follow up with me. Mary kept me updated on Jerome's condition, but there was nothing more I could do at the hospital. I was content to go back to my hotel and rest. I closed it for a couple of days and hired a cleaning service to come in and clean the bloody room."

"Why do you think Harvey stopped to help Jerome? Other people saw him and passed on by."

She thought for a minute. "Honestly, I don't know. Smythville is a very conservative town, and in these parts we don't take kindly to strangers, much less to, you know, his type. But I think he was so full of compassion that his instincts took over, and his own safety and comfort were the last thing on his mind. The most important thing to Harvey was helping Jerome."

Lydia shook her head. "He never told me if he recognized Jerome from the man's political exploits, but if he knew who he was, I would be shocked at the sacrifices Harvey made to help him anyway."

I finished writing my notes, turned off the recording on my phone, and thanked her.

"If you get into contact with Harvey, tell him thank you from me," Lydia requested.

"I will," I promised, closing my notebook. "Are you going to visit Jerome in the rehab clinic today?"

She nodded. "I'll stop in and say hello. I've been checking on his progress on and off. But then I have to get back to my hotel."

I said good-bye to Mary as well, and as I left, I looked back and saw the two of them sharing a hug. I smiled to myself and kept walking. I had an email to send.

chapter six

The Hero

*"But a Samaritan, who was on a journey, came upon him; and when
he saw him, he felt compassion, and came to him and bandaged
up his wounds, pouring oil and wine on them; and he put him on
his own beast, and brought him to an inn and took care of him."*

LUKE 10:33–34 NASB

I went back home and made myself a cup of coffee. I took it to
the back porch and started my email to Harvey:

Hello, Harvey,

*My name is Julie. I am an investigative reporter for The
Journal. I am currently working on a piece about the POTG*

club. In my findings, I came across a victim by the name of Jerome Gorinski, who was brutally beaten and left for dead by the side of Route 8 about two months ago. I spoke to both Mr. Gorinski and the woman, Lydia, who brought him into the ER. In both of their accounts, they cite you as his savior. I am trying to get an accurate account of exactly what happened that night. Would you be open to an interview? I would love to hear your side of the story.

Thank you so much,
Julie Schafer

I sent the email and sat back in my chair, looking up at the sky and letting the sun warm my face. I wanted this interview. Harvey had saved Jerome, and I wanted to know why. If our conversation went well, he could even become the subject of my article.

I thought about the interviews I had conducted so far. Jerome's had been the most shocking, but Pastor Liam's was the hardest for me. He had hurt my family very much, and I was having a hard time forgiving him. In fact, I didn't want to forgive him. Yet I felt God nudging me, so I began to pray. My mother always said that we should bless those whom we have a hard time forgiving, so I began to bless him. As I did, I felt better about the situation, and I knew that even though I couldn't exactly forgive and forget, God was still with me.

Ten minutes later my laptop dinged, pulling me out of my thoughts. I was excited to see that Harvey had responded.

Julie,

I appreciate you reaching out. Unfortunately, I currently don't have a phone, so I can't speak with you. But if you send me a list of questions, I'll email you back with the answers. However, I would like my name and personal information to remain off the record. I'm fine with letting you know the extent of Jerome's injuries, but I wish to remain as anonymous as possible.

Thanks,
Harvey

This was tricky. I wished I could meet up with Harvey, ask him the probing questions, really dig into the story, but that wasn't an option. I emailed him back and let him know that I needed an account of the night he had helped Jerome, with as many details as possible. Why was he driving down that road? What did he do when he found Jerome? Why did he leave so early the next morning? Most importantly, why did he stop to help Jerome in the first place? I also told him that he could be as honest with me as he wanted.

I waited with my laptop open all night, but no email came through. The next day, I distracted myself by typing up Kara and Lydia's stories. Then I printed out the *Gazette* piece. I was standing by my stovetop, thinking about burning that article, when my laptop screen lit up. I ran to the dining table and clicked on my email. Harvey had emailed me back, and it was a long one. I grabbed my water bottle and sat at the table.

Julie,

I think about that night a lot. I've been keeping my eyes out for any information in the news, but there hasn't been any coverage in weeks. When I found Jerome, it was after dark. I was on my way to meet the parents of my then-boyfriend. His parents live around the Smythville area, but we lived in the capital, so it was a bit of a long drive. From what my ex-boyfriend told me, the people in the town are uncomfortable with anything new or different. They are also very conservative, with strong opinions about hot-topic issues. I am both gay and undocumented, so I was very nervous about meeting his parents, and I was anxious to get in and out of the town as quickly as possible.

I was driving down that night after the sun had set, when I saw what I thought was roadkill ahead of me. I slowed down to avoid a pothole in the road, and I saw some clothes in my headlights, and a lot of blood. I pulled my truck over and jumped out, leaving the truck running with the lights on. That's when I saw him. I recognized Jerome immediately. (I'm a big MMA fan.) But before I could even formulate an opinion, I noticed his wounds.

Growing up, I had always wanted to be a doctor, but we couldn't afford school. So I came to America on a temporary worker's visa to be a paramedic. My visa was for three years, but when it expired, I couldn't afford to renew it. I would have had to go back home, and that wasn't an option for me. So I stayed in the U.S. I had a great community here, and this had become home. I had to make some adjustments—I try to avoid the police, any government workers and all potentially hairy situations. But when I saw Jerome, my paramedic training took over and I jumped into action.

I had a bottle of tequila in my truck that I was saving for a special occasion. I grabbed that, my water bottle and my basic first-aid kit that I kept in my car. I turned on my phone's flashlight and began to assess the damage. I had never seen anything like Jerome's injuries before. When I first saw him, I thought he was dead. Then I saw his chest heaving with labored breaths, and when I felt for his pulse, it was weak, but there. The first thing I noticed was his leg. His left tibia had been broken in half, and the lower part of the bone had pierced his skin. I pulled out one of the blankets in the bed of my truck and placed it under the leg. I pulled my belt off and wrapped it around his thigh. He was bleeding at an alarming rate, so I made quick work of securing the makeshift tourniquet and then checking his foot for a pulse. They would have to take X-rays at the hospital, but I hoped he would keep the leg.

Jerome regained consciousness for a second, moaning in pain. When I looked up at his face, I saw his chest. It had been slashed repeatedly, and the letters POTG had been carved into his upper sternum. That's when I knew that this man hadn't been hit by a car or attacked by an animal. A person, or more likely a group, had done this to him. I was almost frozen in anger, but I had a job to do.

As I worked at putting his dislocated arm in a rough sling, Jerome stayed asleep. But when he moaned again, I ripped two packets of ibuprofen open and moved up to his head. I carefully opened his mouth and got him to swallow the four pills with a little bit of water. There was a cut covered in dirt by his eye, so I grabbed my water bottle and emptied it on his face, trying to clean out the wound. Looking down at his body, I knew I would have to get him to someplace safe and clean, with hot running water. I would only be able to do so much with him sprawled in the dirt on the side of the road. The most important thing was to stop any bleeding. I had secured the tourniquet around his leg. His chest wounds would need to be professionally cleaned and stitched.

Jerome was naked, so I grabbed another blanket and covered the lower half of his body. A panic began to set in. I wasn't going to be able to stop all the bleeding here, so I made a decision. I had seen a roadside sign for a hotel about half a mile back. Hopefully, they would let me take care of him there. I knew that I couldn't take him directly to a hospital, because they would ask too many questions. I couldn't risk an encounter with the police because of my citizenship status.

I had a sheet of plywood in the bed of my truck, and I put the last blanket down on top of it. I had some bungee cords, which I hooked to one side of my truck. I jumped in and backed the truck up, stopping when the back tires rolled off the pavement and onto the gravel. I looked up and down the road, double-checking for headlights, before I got out, leaving the truck running. I got out and looked at my setup. Jerome's body was very broken and large, and I'm not the strongest guy in the world. I had a moment of doubt, where I didn't know if I would be able to lift him into the truck safely. I sent up a prayer and bent down to pick him up. I put one arm under his shoulder and one arm under his thigh, on the leg without the tourniquet. I have no idea how I was able to lift him up—maybe God. Yet I managed to get his head and chest onto the plywood with the blanket on it. I began to scoot him up into the truck, eventually pushing on his good leg to shove him all the way in.

I jumped up, rewrapped Jerome's middle, and lashed him to the trunk bed with the bungee cords. Hopping out, I closed the tailgate and ran to the driver's side. I took off down the road, avoiding the pothole and accelerating as fast as possible. Every second of that drive felt like an eternity, and when I finally pulled up to the hotel, I was still running on adrenaline.

I ran in and grabbed the luggage cart. The woman at the counter, Lydia, followed me outside. I remember asking if she had any medical training, and she nodded. Or maybe she asked me? The whole thing feels almost like a fever dream. Together, we managed to keep Jerome steady and get him onto the luggage cart. I wheeled him into a room, and from then on it's a bit of a blur. I remember cleaning his head wounds again and bandaging them up. I remember that the smell of eucalyptus and whiskey was heavy in the room as I worked my way through his injuries. Lydia called 911, but they couldn't make it to us anytime soon. So we did the best we could.

Lydia's nursing bag was a lifesaver. I was able to roughly stitch up the laceration by his eye. I didn't want to touch his chest; there were too many cuts, too deep. Thankfully, Lydia saw to that, and we worked in relative silence. I remember asking her for ice, but mostly she handed me bandages, brought me clean water, and kept trying to force water down Jerome's throat. At one point, we had to hold him down as he screamed in pain. I will never get that sound out of my head! It haunts me to this day.

I couldn't do anything for Jerome's crushed hand, but I was able to control the bleeding around his head and eyes, and Lydia got some more pain pills in him. As we finally reached a place where he was relatively stable, I dabbed her salve onto the cut by his eye and covered it with gauze. Lydia crooked her finger, and we walked out to the desk. I looked down and saw that my favorite shirt was soaked in blood. I smelled like liquor and sweat, but at least Jerome was stable.

Looking around the lobby, I realized that I was in a little gem of a boutique hotel. It looked like this sweet, older woman had decorated it herself, with cheery yellow wallpaper and lots of exposed wood—wooden floors, wooden chairs, wooden beams in the ceiling. I fumbled for my wallet as she pulled up the check-in form on her computer.

Lydia started asking me the typical check-in questions, but normally I don't ever give my real name. I put my arms on the desk and put my head in them. I didn't have the energy to lie to this woman. My adrenaline rush had ended, and I needed some sleep! It was crucial for me to be out of this hotel before the ambulance arrived in the morning, so I told her the truth about my situation.

Lydia went quiet after hearing what I had to say, and I felt a rush of gratitude when she finally asked how long I planned to stay. I gave her enough cash for two nights. I wasn't going to be here tomorrow, but she would have to pay to get the whole room cleaned. I also left my email address, asking her to let me know if she needed any more money, and I would find a way to pay her.

I went back to Jerome's room and watched him sleep. Then I dozed off myself for a couple of hours before I jerked awake. The first thing I saw was that Jerome was still passed out. I felt his forehead for a fever, but it was just clammy and sweaty. I looked at my watch. It was 5 a.m., time to go. I said a hurried good-bye to Lydia and got back on the road. As I drove, I began to cry. I hadn't cried in years, not since I left my parents' home, but I had been through a lot that night. It felt good to get it all out.

I had left my phone back where I found the body, but there was no way that I was going back to get it. I would get a new one, eventually. I needed to get out of this area and go home. I went back to the capital city, and soon after, I decided to move. I wanted to start over by myself somewhere new, *so I left. I wasn't satisfied with my life anymore, and I decided to go looking for something else. Something about that night changed me, but I'm not sure how, exactly.*

You asked me why I helped Jerome. Honestly, I did it because it was the right thing to do. He was dying, and he needed help. It's pretty simple.

Thank you for reaching out, Julie. I was feeling as if I didn't have closure on the whole situation. But now, I can leave it in the past and move on.

Harvey

I sat back and took a deep breath. Wow, I had not expected that. I had wanted a story where Harvey chose to be the bigger person and make a statement or something. But the truth is, he didn't really care about all that. He just did what he thought was right.

I wrote him back a quick thank-you email, promising to keep him anonymous, and adding a quick hello from Lydia. I added his email to my notes for the article. Then I took the rest of that day off. I needed to rest. Emotionally, these last few days had been a lot. I was getting lost in the story, and that wasn't good. I needed to reestablish my journalistic integrity.

I called my dad, who talked my ear off about his new book on American colonialism. Then I drew myself a bath. As I sat in the bubbles, I started processing all I had heard and read. I cried for Jerome and what he had gone through, and I started thinking about what I was going to do next. Whenever I was working on a story, I tried to give every part to God along the way. But the gravity of what had happened to this man was just overwhelming.

Why is this happening, God? I called out, tears running down my face.

In that moment, I felt His presence settle on me, thick and heavy but incredibly light at the same time. Like a whisper in my soul, I felt His voice say, *I am still good.*

I pulled my knees up and put my forehead on them. He was right. I remembered Job and how he had asked the Lord question after question. Instead of answering the questions, God reminded him of just how powerful He is. I needed to refocus my priorities. Bad things happened all the time, but my job wasn't to fix everything, or to understand why things happened the way they did. My job was to be obedient. This reminder, that God was still good, echoed in me as I sat brushing my hair. He was still God, and He was still good.

I took a deep breath and thought about my next steps for the story. The last piece of my puzzle was the POTG club itself. I had to find its leader, Jupiter.

My phone started buzzing. An unknown number was calling me. My heart started pounding, but I answered it with a careful, "Hello?"

"Julie," said the woman at the other end of the line, "I need you to come to the police station." It was Frances, the big-city PR director at the SPD.

"Why?" I asked.

"We've made an arrest, and the woman is asking to speak to you. Apparently, she has ties to the POTG club."

I almost dropped my phone. "She asked to speak to *me* specifically?"

"Yes, but I want to talk to you before you interview her, so hurry over!" Frances snapped, as if she felt irritated to have to include me at all. Then I heard her take a breath. "I'm sorry," she said, "but this last week has been horrific. Can you just get over here fast?"

I assured her that I would be there as quickly as I could and rushed into my bedroom. I threw on my sweatpants and ratty sweatshirt and sprinted out the door, grabbing my notebook and unlocking my car. *Who is this woman they have in custody?* I wondered. *And why does she want to talk to me?*

chapter seven

The Bandit

*"A Jewish man was traveling from Jerusalem down to Jericho,
and he was attacked by bandits. They stripped him of his
clothes, beat him up, and left him half dead beside the road."*

LUKE 10:30 NLT

I arrived at the police station and walked in, pulling out my
phone and checking the charge. I had about 50 percent left;
hopefully it was enough to get me through recording this interview. Frances was waiting for me in the lobby, but this time she
was in sneakers and jeans rather than her glitzy PR setup. *Small
town life must be getting to her*, I thought.

She started walking, and as we made our way down the
hallway, she told me what had happened. The police had been

following up on a report that there was a drug deal going down at a local martial arts gym. When they pulled up, no one was there, but they found a charm bracelet with the letter *S* on it that had been left at the crime scene.

Frances sighed. "We asked the local jeweler who had purchased it, which led us to Savannah. When we brought her in, she didn't ask for a lawyer or anything. She just said, 'I know who the leader of the POTG club is, and I will only speak to Julie, the reporter.' We kept asking her questions, but that's all she would say. We don't have much time left before we have to release her, and we need her to talk."

I nodded. When I was coming up as a journalist in the city, one of my mentors told me about a serial killer in police custody he had interviewed. The man would only speak with a reporter, because he wanted to be famous. A lot of creeps wanted to confess, but only on their own terms.

We reached the end of the hallway, where a set of doors waited for us on the left. The closest one was open, and a group of police officers waited inside.

"Julie," said Frances, "good luck!"

I walked into the next room, not knowing what to expect. A young woman sat at the table. She was maybe in her late twenties and was wearing a dirty sundress. Her hair looked as though it had once been immaculately curled, but it now hung in limp waves down her back. When I came in, she turned to look at me, and I shivered. The woman who sat before me was broken—that much was clear.

"Julie?" she asked.

I nodded and sat down in the freezing metal chair across from her.

"Is it alright with you if I record this?" I asked.

She shook her head yes and tossed her hair over her shoulders, a difficult maneuver since her hands were cuffed to the desk.

"Savannah?" I asked, starting the recording and putting my phone down, "Where do you want to start?"

She gave me a slow, mean smile and began: "About a year ago, I was walking down the road when a man on a motorcycle pulled up next to me and offered me a ride. He was so hot, and the bike was cool, so I hopped on. He drove me around town, and we finally stopped for a bite to eat. He had this dangerous edge to him that I liked, because it was new and different. We started hanging out more and more, and pretty soon I had fallen in love with him."

"What did your parents think about him?" I asked.

"Well, my father is dead, and my mom doesn't really know about stuff in my life, or care."

I wrote "Mom?" in my notes as she continued.

"Anyway, he introduced himself as Jupiter, and I moved in with him right away. We had so much in common." Her eyes wondered off, and for a minute she looked almost human. "I loved him so much, and he loved me too."

Then she seemed to remember that she was being interviewed, and the cold look came back into her eyes. "Things were perfect. We decided to join a gym together—FFS."

"What's that?" I asked.

"FFS? That's the Fusion Fitness Studio. It's a mixed martial arts gym. In high school, I took self-defense classes, and I loved the intensity of it all. So I started taking Krav Maga. This gym was the best because you could take all different kinds of classes. Jupiter loved boxing, so he and I would go to the gym and take classes. After our class, we would spar with each other." She laughed. "He almost always won, but sometimes he would back off at the last moment and let me win. It was fun."

"So how did the POTG club begin?" I asked.

"Jupiter spent a lot of time online. He had started a forum for guys who liked to fight. Pretty soon, it got out of hand. He had always been kinda crazy, and these guys just seemed to rile him up. He would get into these rants about the police and the courts, and how guilty people kept walking free. There was this story in the news about a guy who was arrested for beating his wife, and I remember Jupiter saying, 'If the police don't do anything about this guy, I will!' Sure enough, when they released the guy a few days later, Jupiter took matters into his own hands. He invited a few guys from the gym over to our place for dinner. We ordered some pizzas, and while they ate, they made a plan. I don't ever remember agreeing to be part of it, but the next thing I knew, we were wearing black masks and driving up to the guy's house."

She went on with the rough part of the story: "Jupiter's friend had this old fifteen-passenger van, so we all fit. When we got to his house, we saw him walk out with a dog on a leash. His wife followed, crying and we watched as he slapped her across the face. I was so mad, and Jupiter looked madder than I had ever seen. The woman went back inside, and he kept walking the dog. When he was a little way from the house, the guys grabbed him and put a bag over his head. We drove to this clearing in the woods, tied him up, and kicked him over and over again. Honestly, it was kind of satisfying. He deserved it, and it was a good feeling to be giving him what he deserved. I had seen so many nasty people walk free, and it felt as if I was doing something worthwhile."

As I listened to Savannah, I felt sick. Although I hadn't interviewed the guy, I had read the story. One of his ribs had punctured his lung, and he had been in the hospital for six weeks in recovery.

"What did Jupiter think about what happened?" I asked.

"Oh, he loved it!" she said, putting her head in her hands. "He wouldn't stop talking about it. The guys all came back to our place afterward to celebrate. That night, he stood up and announced that we were going to start a group, the *Punishers Of The Guilty*. He was pretty drunk, so I tried to laugh it off, but he was serious. He felt as though it was his duty to 'punish the guilty,' and that's what he did."

Savannah explained what had happened next: "We began to watch the news for people to punish, and there were so many. It was my job to choose the people, and Jupiter was the one who chose how we would punish them. I was never really good at school or anything, but I was good at this. Pretty soon, the group started growing. He would troll the internet and invite guys from these crazy online forums to visit, and they would come to Smythville, do a POTG job with us, and then leave. But there's a main group of us who are all local."

"Who are those local people?"

"Well, there's Jupiter and me; we're kinda like the leaders. But the first group was a bunch of guys from the gym, and they pretty much came on every job with us. We all worked out together, and soon we learned each other's fighting styles. Jupiter loved being in charge, and he started to change."

Again I asked, "Who are the local members?"

Savannah laughed coldly, and I shuddered and began praying in my head.

"I'm not telling you," she answered. "But like I said, Jupiter started to change. At first, we were only targeting guys who were on the news. But then, he started asking me to look around town for people who needed punishing. No one was safe. He also started to develop a sick kind of fascination with himself. He had these robes that he made us wear for some of the jobs, and his was different than ours, special. We never wanted to let anyone see our faces, so he bought some crazy masks for us. The guys loved it."

I sighed internally. Savannah only wanted to talk about Jupiter, but at least she was talking.

"What about Jerome Gorinski?" I asked.

"Oh, that was a crazy one. Jupiter decided that we all needed more training, so he started assigning us weapons. He told me to learn how to use a police baton. I felt really dumb holding a freaking police baton!" She rolled her eyes.

"Honestly, the longer this whole thing went on, the stupider I thought the way Jupiter ran things was getting," she admitted. "But I loved doing the jobs because I got to practice my skills and punish the guilty ones. At the gym, Jupiter started training us privately. Pretty soon, he wouldn't let me go to my class or talk to anyone else. He got crazy possessive and toxic. One evening, when he thought the group was ready to practice with weapons outside the gym, we went on a drive. The original plan was that we would try to find a homeless guy and practice on him, but all the guys we saw were in town, so we drove outside town. That's when we saw Jerome Gorinski, the famous MMA fighter, walking by the side of the road. The guys started chanting, and Jupiter pulled the van over in front of him, cutting off his exit. We all got out of the back, and I was feeling the adrenaline. This guy was huge. He looked as if he could take on all of us. I got a little scared, but part of me was also really excited. I hadn't had a chance to challenge myself, especially against a pro like this guy, but here was the perfect opportunity. Jerome looked at us, and Jupiter got out, sliding on his brass knuckles. That's when Jerome looked scared."

Savannah sat back in the seat. "Jupiter's pretty big, too. He's also confident. All the guys loved him, and at that point they would have done anything for him. He always loves to look down on the guilty from up above them, so I moved in quick and hit Jerome's legs and he went down." She shivered. "It's just so satisfying."

"What is?" I prompted her.

"Getting someone down. This guy was probably about twice my size, but in one move I had him on his knees. Jupiter made the guy undress. Then, Jerome lunged for B—I mean, the guy's legs who had the nunchuks."

She had stared to say a name and then caught herself, grinning sheepishly at me. "Before Jerome could do anything, the guy whipped him in the face with the nunchucks, and then we saw the first blood. After that, it turned into a real fight. We all got a chance to practice, but mostly we kept hitting him. Jupiter sat back, playing with his knife and watching. I could see the pride in his eyes when I hit the guy on the back of the head, and then it all went south. Jerome got one of the guys in a sleeper hold, and then I knew Jupiter was going to take care of him. We all mobbed the big guy at once, and he let go. Then Jupiter moved in and carved up the dude's chest while he screamed, and then he knocked him out. He let us go at him again, but we were all pretty exhausted by that time."

She went on filling in the horrifying details: "Jerome was just lying there, and it's no fun to beat up a guy who can't fight back. But Jupiter went totally nuts. He started kicking his ribs and grabbed my baton. He started whacking his shin, and we all heard the bone snap and saw it poke through. At that point, I was done and got back in the van."

She looked sick and swallowed hard. "But Jupiter kept going. That's when I knew something was wrong with him. No one in his right mind just attacks someone like that for no reason—especially some random guy we didn't even have anything against that we needed to punish him for."

I felt the weight of what she had said and let her sit in it for a second. "Were you wearing masks?" I asked.

"No," she said. "We weren't worried about Jerome identifying us, because we knew he was going to die. He was almost dead when we left. Everyone got back in the van, and when Jupiter looked at me, he had this look in his eyes. He was excited, riding a high, and a little reckless. Instead of driving back home right away, he kept driving around town, blasting music."

"What happened when you eventually went home?" I asked.

"Well, it was almost as if an itch had been scratched. Things kind of went back to normal. But Jupiter had changed. He became even more obsessed with the POTG club, and became much more demanding. When he learned that Jerome had lived, he got mad. He wanted me to find more guilty people, and whenever we would punish them, he wanted to make sure they knew our club's name. At first, we left notes stapled to them, or told them to remember us. Then he came up with the insane idea of actually carving our club's initials, POTG, into the people we chose to punish, like he did to Jerome. That would make them remember us for life! At the beginning, the club was supposed to be, like, hidden, but by the time we got to Jerome, the word had started getting out. Instead of backing down, Jupiter started ramping up. He wanted people to know who we were."

"Is that where I came in?" I asked.

"Yes," she said. "He wanted the world to know about us. So he started getting creative with the punishments, making them flashy and memorable. The longer it went on, the more flamboyant they got as Jupiter became obsessed with making sure people would remember us. He found out somehow that you were the reporter working on the story for *The Journal*. But the longer you took digging around without getting our club in the newspaper, the more impatient he got. He wanted you to write the story on us quick!"

"Why me?" I asked. "Why did you ask to talk to me?"

She got a sad smile. "I know the police in this town. I've been cleaning up their messes for the last year. There's no way I trust them. At least as a reporter you have a duty to share the truth."

"Are you afraid of Jupiter?" I asked.

Savannah sighed. "At first I wasn't. It was hot. We were like Bonnie and Clyde. But after Jerome, I didn't want to do it anymore. Jupiter wanted to do it more. I started to get scared that I would be the next victim. Jupiter would get really paranoid if I went anywhere without him, and he started to follow me everywhere I went. If he knew I was telling you my side of the story, I'm pretty sure he would kill me, for real."

I looked up at the mirror in the room and nodded. I grabbed one of her hands. "Thank you for telling me," I told her.

Savannah smiled. The mean look had gone out of her eyes. I felt that in sharing her story with me, she had let a little piece of herself go, and maybe it was a piece that needed to be let go.

"I hope you write a good story," she told me as a police officer opened a door and I got up to leave. Another officer walked in, and as we passed each other on my way out, I looked back at Savannah. What I saw was a scared girl who had gotten in over her head. I sent up a prayer for her, that she would reconnect with her mother. She had told me her mom didn't know what was going on in her life and didn't care, but this "tough" girl obviously still needed mothering. So I sent up a prayer for her mom, too. I hoped Savannah could reconnect with someone who really loved her, and could actually learn how to be happy again.

Frances met me outside the room. I sat back against the wall and slid to the ground. She sat next to me and took a deep breath. "We're going to need the names of the club members," she said.

"She won't give them to you," I replied. "She wouldn't give them to me."

Miss PR department smiled her annoying little smile. "We'll see . . ."

I rolled my eyes. "Did Savannah call anyone?" I asked.

"No, but we called her mother."

I sighed and got up. "That's good! Well, I'm out of here. I need to type up these notes and try to track down Jupiter."

"If we find him, I'll tell you," Frances said. She held out her hand to shake mine.

Surprised, I shook it and thanked her. I walked out to my car. Lost in thought, I didn't even notice that my car was already unlocked. I sat down in the driver's seat, and as I moved to start the car, I felt a cool, sharp metal object press against my throat as a hand covered my mouth.

"Don't move a muscle," said a deep, cold voice.

chapter eight

The Reckoning

*The Light shines in the darkness, and
the darkness did not comprehend it.*
JOHN 1:5 NASB

I sat frozen at the wheel.

"What did that snitch tell you?" The voice hissed into my ear. I flinched as a fleck of spit hit my ear. He removed his hand from my mouth.

"Why do you care?" I asked.

The voice laughed dryly. "Start the car!" he said, moving his knife off my skin but keeping it angled at my throat. I started the car, but kept it in park. My mind was going a million miles a minute. This was obviously Jupiter, or one of his lackeys. There was no way he was getting me to drive to a remote location; I needed to stay right here. I remembered the gun in my center console, and I slowly started reaching for it.

"Are you Jupiter?" I asked, inching my right elbow back to rest on the console.

He laughed again. "Of course I am."

"Why are you doing this?"

As he launched into his tirade, I kept all my focus on slowly moving my hand back and planning my next steps.

"*Because of her!*" he yelled. "I *tried* to keep her safe! I *tried* to protect her, because without me, she's vulnerable. I have to save her!"

"Save her from whom?" I questioned.

"*Save her from THEM!*" he yelled again. "Do you think the police are *innocent*? They're as guilty as the people I punish!"

"What if she's selling you out to them?" I asked, trying to get him even madder so he wouldn't notice what I was doing.

"Impossible! She would never do that!" He argued, his hands shaking.

I saw the reflected light of the blade wobble, and I moved. I reached up my left hand lightning fast and grabbed his wrist, at the same time opening the console with my right hand and grabbing the gun. Startled, he dropped the knife onto my lap as I whipped around and pointed the gun at him. He froze and put both hands up.

"Don't move!" I said as I quickly opened my door and slid out, keeping the gun pointed at him the whole time. The knife dropped harmlessly to the ground.

He moved to open his door.

"*I said don't move!*" I yelled, and he smiled wider, still opening the door. I shot the gun, aiming for the tree across the street. The sound of the gun shocked him into obedience and brought the police running, firearms ready.

"This is the guy—this is Jupiter!" I told the officers, dropping my gun and putting my hands on my head.

"Get on the ground, Julie!" I heard, and I dropped to my knees. One officer came up and handcuffed me, walking me in. I knew he had to do it because he had seen me with a gun in hand, threatening a guy, and he had heard the shot when I fired it. I heard another officer command Jupiter to get out of the car and place his hands on the hood.

Later, after I explained what had happened and gave my official statement, they released me. Each of the officers shook my hand and thanked me.

Frances was waiting for me outside. She offered to drive me home in her hot pink car, and I reluctantly let her. She said I could leave my car at the station and she'd help me get it later. As she drove, I began to process what had happened to me. I started to shake, and she grabbed my hand.

"You're okay," she said. "Take a breath."

I took a shaky breath and placed my hands on her dashboard. She began to pray in tongues, out loud, as I took deep breaths. I felt comforted as her prayers washed over me. As upset as I was over the whole incident, I still remember thinking, *There's more to this lady than meets the eye. She knows the Holy Spirit too!*

When we arrived at my house, Frances walked around her car, opened the door, and walked me inside. She went around locking my back door and all the windows. I sat on my couch, still shaking, and she wrapped a blanket around me. She also offered to get me something hot to drink and sat with me for a few minutes while I sipped it, until she was sure I had calmed down. Then knowing that I was absolutely exhausted, she got ready to leave. "Call me anytime," she said as she exited through my front door.

I got up to lock the door behind her, and then I collapsed back onto the couch. I fell asleep almost immediately and slept for the next thirteen hours.

The next morning, I got up and made some coffee, replaying the events of the day before in my head. I texted Molly, the victim who had tipped me off about Jerome, to let her know that the police had the leader of the POTG club in custody. Then I sat down at my desk. It was time to get to work . . .

chapter nine

The End and a Beginning

*Be diligent to present yourself approved to God
as a workman who does not need to be ashamed,
accurately handling the word of truth.*

2 TIMOTHY 2:15 NASB

It had been a month and a half since my story broke. As I sat on my porch and looked out at the hummingbirds hovering around the feeder, I thought about the process. I had moved back home to Smythville for a slower life, but instead, this story had found me. Jupiter had agreed to give me an exclusive interview from prison. That had been difficult for me after feeling his knife at my throat in the car. But I got past it, determined to finish the story I had been working so hard on, even finding myself in danger over it. His story aligned with Savannah's, mostly.

I shivered a little, remembering that scenario in my car with him. Jupiter still gave me the creeps, even though he was now behind bars. It turned out that due to the severity of his crimes and the publicity this case had warranted, the District Attorney chose to try the case at the state courthouse. It was taking the DA's office some time to build a case against Jupiter, but he was in custody, and the town he had terrorized was safe from him again. The DA had offered Savannah a plea bargain, and she was going to take it. Her trial was scheduled to start this afternoon.

I thought about all the people who stood out throughout this investigation. Although my article focused on the POTG club itself, Jerome's story was the one that had stayed with me. Jerome had recently been released from the hospital. He had called a press conference to announce that he was leaving the world of MMA. Instead, he announced, he was going to be starting a nonprofit gym that would help boys and young men who were in difficult situations learn how to handle their emotions in healthy ways.

I emailed Harvey a copy of my *Journal* article when it came out, but he never responded, nor did I expect him to. I was glad that he had found closure, and I prayed every day for him to have peace, wherever he was.

I also caught up with Kara, the girl who volunteered at her church so much but who had passed by Jerome on that dark night, worried for her own safety. She had gotten back with her boyfriend, and she confided to me that she had also started going to weekly therapy. We had become close as I got to know her better, and she was my new prayer partner. We were learning a lot from each other about living out our faith. I sent her a quick text, asking her if I could pray for her.

Soon after my article was published in *The Journal*, Pastor Liam and his wife moved to Europe. He wanted to pursue a career in higher education, and I privately thought that teaching would suit him better than pastoring. Their replacement was a couple who were some of the kindest people I had ever met. I had forgiven Pastor Liam, but that didn't mean that I had to be pastored by him. The new couple were so gentle with our town as we all healed, and they brought such life and joy to their church services every week.

Kara and I were going to Fellowship Church together now, and this week Molly, the victim who used to be a prostitute, would be joining us. Molly didn't end up leaving town. She stayed and started working for Lydia at the Samaritan Hotel. However, Frances, the police department's PR rep, did go back to her big-city job. She and I were on good terms when she left. We had discovered that we had our faith in common, and she had been so caring toward me after the incident of Jupiter trying to hold me hostage in my car.

As for Lydia and her daughter, Nurse Mary, that would be a story for another time. I shook my head.

My phone buzzed in my hand, and I saw that Pops was calling me.

"*Hi, Pops!*" I yelled into the phone.

"*Hi, Sugar!*" he yelled back. "I'm reading your *Journal* story again right now. This is amazing, Sweetie! I'm so proud of you!"

I smiled. No matter how many times he told me, it made me smile every time. "Thanks, Pops!" I said.

"What is my ace reporter of a granddaughter working on these days?" he asked.

"I'm not sure. But Mark is supposed to call me later today with my next assignment."

"That's really good. *I love you, Sugar!*" he yelled into the phone.

I blew kisses into the phone and hung up. Mark had loved my POTG story. He had loved it even more when the story went viral, the digital copy getting over 10 million hits in the first week. I had declined every offer to appear publicly, asking Mark to handle it all. He had gladly agreed, and our subscriber list had skyrocketed worldwide.

My phone buzzed again. It was Mark this time.

"Talk to me," I said.

"Oh, Julie," he said excitedly, "I've got a good one for you!"

I pulled out my notepad and started taking notes, ready for whatever the next assignment brought.

"The Punishers Are the Guilty"

By Julie Schafer

It was 7 o'clock, and the night nurses had just arrived. The girl walked into the ER, carrying her own thumb in a plastic baggie. In the chaos that followed, one of the nurses remembers her saying, "It was the POTG!"

In Smythville, things are normally quiet. The locals are proud of their tranquil lives, but even more proud of their town's yearly apple pie contest that the mayor's wife inevitably wins. But this rose-colored town has been shadowed by a dark evil for more than a year.

The Punishers Of The Guilty, or POTG, is a vigilante group whose members decided to take the justice system of the town into their own hands. One victim remembers the club's leader saying, "We *have found you guilty!*" before the group enacted their "punishment."

"Linda," a local former prostitute who was another victim, was admitted to the ER with severe wounds to her genitalia and a note stappled to her breast that read *Compliments of the POTG*. When "Linda" spoke to *The Journal*, she told of a cult-like group whose members wore black robes and black masks and chanted during their attacks on people. This ritualized violence was a cornerstone of the organization, as they dealt out guilty verdicts and "matched" their punishments accordingly. The girl with her thumb in a baggie was a known pickpocketer. The POTG had also attempted to castrate a rapist, and they had shaved the head and disfigured the face of a young beauty queen who had slept her way to a victory.

These are just some of the horrific crimes committed by the POTG club, all under the leadership of a man named Jupiter. Jupiter had started the group over a year ago when he became disillusioned with the local police, who had released a man who was a known abuser. According to the POTG leader's then-girlfriend, Savannah, Jupiter had heard about it and said, "If the police don't do anything about this guy, I will!"

Then he did. He and his girlfriend were regulars at the local gym, frequenting classes like Krav Maga (Savannah) and boxing (Jupiter). Some of the friends he made came to his house for dinner one night, where they formulated a plan. They proceeded to kidnap and assault the released abuser, whom they caught in the act of abusing his wife again in the couple's home.

These vigilantes claimed that the man deserved every blow. That night, Jupiter named their group the POTG, for Punishers Of The Guilty, and their reign of terror began.

According to Savannah, Jupiter soon began chatting online with like-minded people across the country who wanted to take justice into their own hands. These people would travel from their homes in other states to assist Jupiter in carrying out his "punishments." Why would anyone travel such distances to join in one man's vendetta against one town?

The answer lies within Jupiter himself. *Charismatic*, *charming*, and *persuasive* are all traits that members of various cults use to describe their leaders. Jupiter possesses each of these traits, along with a ruthless attitude toward meting out justice. Although he held no religious sway over the individuals who became involved with the POTG, his opinionated rants, calls for justice, and ability to unite the group under a common goal are what made this group as destructive as they were. He was able to take the core group of four men and his girlfriend and essentially get them to do whatever he wanted, plus convince others far outside Smythville to come join them in taking the law into their own hands. He even hoped his movement would spread when outsiders saw what the POTG was doing in Smythville and took it back to their own communities.

Many criminals with violent tendencies crave an escalation. Expert psychologists have explained that often, violent criminals are chasing a sort of "high." The first time they commit an act of violence, it gives them a rush of adrenaline, and they become addicted to trying to replicate that. In Jupiter's case, it seems he became addicted to a feeling of power and control. As the town's residents became more and more fearful, he was planning something bigger. In an exclusive interview from his jail cell, Jupiter admitted that he wanted to test his group's loyalty to him. "I wanted to know if they would do what I asked, even if the person was innocent," he told *The Journal*.

This led to a brutal attack on Jerome Gorinski, a former MMA expert well-known for his fighting abilities. One night when he was walking alongside the county road just outside Smythville, Route 8, Jerome was beaten within an inch of his life and left for dead, which was Jupiter's goal all along. "I wanted to know what it felt like to have someone die at my command," Jupiter admitted.

Besides himself, the key players in Gorinski's tale include a local pastor, a frightened onlooker, a local hotel owner, and a heroic stranger who saved him. The compilation of all the parties' accounts who were involved on that night reveals a shocking and heart-wrenching story. Savannah recalled how the POTG beat Gorinski and left him for dead on the side of the road. As Gorinski lay dying, a minister passed by who offered prayers for his safety from the car but who never got out. Shortly afterward, a young woman was stranded on Route 8 with a flat tire. Seeing signs of a bloody attack near her car and fearing for her own life, she changed her tire and left quickly. Not much later, a young man traveling near Smythville happened upon Gorinski's body. Using his paramedic training, this young man was able to save Jerome's life and move him to a local hotel, where the innkeeper, a former nurse, assisted in performing lifesaving first aid. This heroic stranger left the next day, entrusting Jerome to the care of the woman who owned the hotel. She oversaw his admission to the hospital. Although it appears that Gorinski and the young man who saved him have diametrically opposed lifestyles and political views, this young man saved Jerome's life "because it was the right thing to do."

Gorinski was admitted to the hospital with devastating wounds, along with the letters *POTG* carved into his chest with a knife. When this particular detail hit the newsstands, Jerome's story became a brief national sensation. And Jupiter, the club's leader, became more obsessed. The crimes his group committed would always include either notes referencing the group (like the POTG note stapled to "Linda's" breast) or horrifying stories of the group torturing their victims while chanting their club name, so all the victims could remember was "Punishers Of The Guilty."

The POTG's increase in visibility was not the only thing that changed for the group over time. The club was unified under a common goal of "serving justice." However, after the attack on Gorinski, apparently its members were feeling less unified. Savannah, one of the self-described "leaders" of the core group and its only female, was severely disturbed at what they had done to an innocent man, Jerome, and became less and less enthusiastic. When she was eventually arrested in connection with a potential drug bust, she admitted to being involved in the POTG club and confessed what they had done. She was fearful for her life, telling a *Journal* reporter, "If Jupiter knew I was telling this story, he would kill me, for real."

The night of Savannah's arrest, Jupiter was also caught. He had broken into the same reporter's car, holding her at knifepoint, before being apprehended by nearby police officers. His obsession with public image and notoriety led him to give this reporter an exclusive interview from behind bars. He also disclosed the identities of his loyal devotees.

Up until now, the unwritten part of this story has lain behind the courts. This violent club started because some citizens with violent tendencies felt there was an unsatisfactory legal response to the crimes taking place in Smythville. When the *Journal* spoke to a local judge, the Honorable Justice Finley Johnson, he commented that due to overcrowding in the prisons, in lieu of incarceration he was being pushed to deliver sentences that sent criminals to rehabilitation or meted out larger amounts of community service. Because of this, many offenders were being released on parole, continuing the cycle. Many of those released on parole were nonviolent criminals who went on to live peaceful lives. Yet the cruel reality is that when placed back into a stressful environment, a large number of these men and women fell back into their old illegal pursuits. Hence, the desire of the POTG to deliver its own brand of "justice."

Due to the gravity and severity of his crimes, Jupiter is being charged by the DA on 70 counts of criminal assault and battery, 3 counts of rape, 1 count of attempted manslaughter, and 1 count of domestic abuse. Jupiter seems smug about the whole operation. "They've let worse men than me walk," he told *The Journal* in his interview. His trial has been moved to the state courthouse, and from his jail cell he awaits his day in court.

Speaking to *The Journal* about this group, many locals expressed relief that the POTG club had disbanded. However, some were slightly disappointed. "Don't get me wrong," said one Smythville local who asked to remain anonymous. "I think what the POTG did was wrong. But I have to say, I don't disagree with why they did it."

While this attitude is not shared by many, it is shared by enough citizens to make the Smythville Police Department concerned. A representative from the SPD issued a public apology shortly following the arrest of both Savannah and Jupiter, stating, "We want to reiterate that the acts the POTG club committed are serious crimes, and we will seek to bring justice for all their victims. We also want to assure the community that, in light of the current attitude of some toward Smythville's police and justice system, we are working as hard as we can to maintain a safe community, where you can trust your police department to keep you and your loved ones secure."

In the wake of the POTG atrocities and arrests, Smythville is slowly returning to normal. The club's victims who were in long-term rehabilitation are returning to their families. Those who needed psychological help are receiving it. Those who were criminals unwilling to change their ways or apologize are receiving their just desserts. For example, the POTG's first victim, the wife abuser, left the hospital only to find that his wife and children had moved away, leaving him to nurse his wounds alone. When contacted by *The Journal*, he declined to comment.

As Smythville heals from these horrors, a new spirit of camaraderie has taken root in the town, one that is almost diametrically opposite the sick loyalty that Jupiter demanded from his followers. The townspeople are relying on each other, sharing their fears, taking care of those who need help, and working to establish their town as a pleasant place to live. The icing on the proverbial cake was the latest apple pie contest, where this time the winner was "Linda," the victim who has left her former life of prostitution. She now works in hospitality and has taken to maintaining a close relationship with the local police department.

As for Jerome, the victim who committed no crimes yet still suffered a POTG attack, he has started his own gym, training boys and young men to learn how to handle their emotions in a healthy way. He sends his thanks to his saviors and asks the reader to remember that extending compassion to someone can mean the difference between life and death.

Conclusion

As you've finished reading this book, it's our prayer that you have experienced God's presence and healing for the trauma ripples that you may have experienced personally or from others. God uses a variety of methods and timings for healing—sometimes God heals instantly, and sometimes God's healing is a gradual progression. It's also interesting to consider that God uses a wide array of situations, people, tools, conversations, surprises, etc. to continue healing in our lives and the lives of others.

For example, I'll never forget receiving a letter from a person who heard me give a sermon when I had a meltdown. I remember that I was really embarrassed by my breakdown and wished that I'd maintained my composure better. The letter I received compassionately acknowledged what happened in my sermon, and the woman who wrote it said that she thought she could help me. At first, I was taken aback that someone would follow up on my meltdown, but I contacted the woman and started a very helpful therapy journey where I began to sort out various traumas and impacts in my life.

In terms of helping someone recover from trauma, I can see myself in the various characters in the Good Samaritan parable. I suspect that you may also see yourself as each individual in the parable, in various situations and seasons in your life.

With all of these things in mind, let's keep our focus square on Jesus' words in John 10:10 (NASB), *"The thief comes only to steal and kill and destroy; I came that they may have life, and have it abundantly."*

This verse reminds us that the enemy of our soul wants to do nothing but hurt and destroy us. In contrast, Jesus wants to give us abundant life. To this end, let's continue to let Jesus work in our souls, redeeming and transforming traumas that we've experienced. Let's also give Jesus permission to use us as a tool to heal and redeem traumas that others have experienced.

For some concluding ideas and exercises, consider going through the worksheets again at the end of each chapter for the non-fiction content in this book.

epilogue

Below, you will find verses that could be helpful on your road to wholeness. You could employ these verses in a variety of ways, and here are a few suggestions:

- Memorize one verse each week and let it be a grounding point for your thoughts and focus when you find yourself struggling with various traumas.

- Keep these verses in your phone (on the notes, in a picture, etc) for easy reference as you go about your day.

- Pray these verses over yourself each morning before you begin the activities of your day.

- Share these verses with a friend or in a small group and have some conversation around them.

- Review the context of each verse and think about how you can relate to these various contexts.

- Ask God to highlight one of these verses for you to absorb and fully permeate your soul.

- Make an audio memo on your phone, reading these verses aloud so you can play them back to yourself in key moments, throughout the day and/or to help you with remembering them.

Verses:

Lamentations 3:21–24, *"This I recall to my mind, Therefore I have hope. The* LORD's *lovingkindnesses indeed never cease, for His compassions never fail. They are new every morning; Great is Your faithfulness. "The* LORD *is my portion," says my soul, "Therefore I have hope in Him"* (NASB).

Isaiah 41:10, *"Do not fear, for I am with you; do not anxiously look about you, for I am your God. I will strengthen you, surely I will help you, surely I will uphold you with My righteous right hand"* (NASB).

Psalm 34:18, *The* LORD *is near to the brokenhearted and saves those who are crushed in spirit* (NASB).

John 16:33, *"These things I have spoken to you, so that in Me you may have peace. In the world you have tribulation, but take courage; I have overcome the world"* (NASB).

Isaiah 26:3–4, *"The steadfast of mind You will keep in perfect peace, because he trusts in You. Trust in the* Lord *forever, for in* God *the* Lord, *we have an everlasting Rock"* (NASB).

2 Corinthians 1:3–4, *Blessed be the God and Father of our Lord Jesus Christ, the Father of mercies and God of all comfort, who comforts us in all our affliction so that we will be able to comfort those who are in any affliction with the comfort with which we ourselves are comforted by God* (NASB).

Romans 15:13, *Now may the God of hope fill you with all joy and peace in believing, so that you will abound in hope by the power of the Holy Spirit* (NASB).

Philippians 4:6–7, *Be anxious for nothing, but in everything by prayer and supplication with thanksgiving let your requests be made known to God. And the peace of God, which surpasses all comprehension, will guard your hearts and your minds in Christ Jesus* (NASB).

Ephesians 1:18–19, *I pray that the eyes of your heart may be enlightened, so that you will know what is the hope of His calling, what are the riches of the glory of His inheritance in the saints, and what is the surpassing greatness of His power toward us who believe. These are in accordance with the working of the strength of His might* (NASB).

Ephesians 3:16–19, *That He would grant you, according to the riches of His glory, to be strengthened with power through His Spirit in the inner man, so that Christ may dwell in your hearts through faith; and that you, being rooted and grounded in love, may be able to comprehend with all the saints what is the breadth and length and height and depth, and to know the love of Christ which surpasses knowledge, that you may be filled up to all the fullness of God* (NASB).

1 John 4:16, *We have come to know and have believed the love which God has for us. God is love, and the one who abides in love abides in God, and God abides in him* (NASB).

Jeremiah 17:14, *Heal me, O LORD, and I will be healed; save me and I will be saved, for You are my praise* (NASB).

Matthew 6:14, *"For if you forgive others for their transgressions, your heavenly Father will also forgive you"* (NASB).

Psalm 46:1–2, *God is our refuge and strength, a very present help in trouble. Therefore we will not fear, though the earth should change and though the mountains slip into the heart of the sea* (NASB).

Luke 10:33–34, *"But a Samaritan, who was on a journey, came upon him; and when he saw him, he felt compassion, and came to him and bandaged up his wounds, pouring oil and wine on them; and he put him on his own beast, and brought him to an inn and took care of him"* (NASB).

Romans 8:26, *In the same way the Spirit also helps our weakness; for we do not know how to pray as we should, but the Spirit Himself intercedes for us with groanings too deep for words* (NASB).

Psalm 118:5–6, *From my distress I called upon the* Lord; *the* Lord *answered me and set me in a large place. The* Lord *is for me; I will not fear; what can man do to me?* (NASB).

Additionally, here are some further resources that could be helpful:

- *The Body Keeps the Score: Brain, Mind, and Body in the Healing of Trauma* by Bessel van der Kolk M.D.

- *Cleaning Up Your Mental Mess: 5 Simple, Scientifically Proven Steps to Reduce Anxiety, Stress, and Toxic Thinking* by Dr. Caroline Leaf

- *Changes That Heal: Four Practical Steps to a Happier, Healthier You* by Dr. Henry Cloud

- *The Inner Voice of Love: A Journey Through Anguish to Freedom* by Henri Nouwen

acknowledgements

Writing a book is a gigantic undertaking, and loads of people contribute in a variety of ways to make an outcome that's helpful for readers. Thank you to everyone who contributed to this project, with special gratitude to Isabell, Sarah, Diane, Lori, Terry, Brenda, Brooke, and most of all, Jesus!

SARAH

I want to thank every single person who helped me make this dream a reality. Thank you, Mom, for letting me join you; Aunt Diane for your wisdom, Sarah Heaton for your direction; and my editor, Trish, for every single thing you did. Y'all rock!

For all of the 5 Families Girls: chosen sisters are for life, and no one has supported me better than you. I love you so much!

For my ORU Friends and Family: I've said it once, and I'll say it again: without you, I wouldn't be here. Thank you, thank you, thank you.

For Jesus: my Love and my Lord. I adore you.

ISABELL

Sarah Bowling

Sarah Bowling is on a mission to connect every one with the heart of God while loving those who are overlooked, excluded, and ignored. Led by Holy Spirit and anchored in the Word, Sarah seeks to inspire all to know the unconditional and transformational love of God in our daily lives. She is a discerning Bible teacher, an international speaker and a global humanitarian.

As part of *Marilyn & Sarah Ministries*, Sarah co-hosts a daily television program, *Today with Marilyn & Sarah*, reaching a potential daily audience of 2.2 billion households worldwide. Sarah has been a key-note speaker at events all over the world and has also authored numerous books, including *In Step with the Spirit, Hey God, Can We Talk?*, and *Your Friendship with Holy Spirit*.

Sarah is the founder of *Saving Moses*, a global humanitarian organization saving babies (5 and under) every day by meeting the most urgent and intense survival needs where help is least available. Saving Moses funds and establishes revolutionary programs in nations of the world that record the highest infant mortality rate and where babies of sex workers are most susceptible to exploitation.

Through her books, blogs, podcasts, videos, and live teaching events, Sarah is committed to sharing life-giving revelation that will transform lives on a daily basis.

Sarah and her husband, Reece, have three children and are Lead Pastors of Encounter Church in Denver, Colorado. She holds a Bachelor of Arts degree from Oral Roberts University and a Master of Arts degree from the University of Missouri.

Isabell Bowling

Growing up under the teachings of her grandmother and mom, Isabell developed a passion for the Word and for loving people well at an early age. When mental health issues and church hurt caused her to doubt her faith, God brought her back into His loving embrace.

In 2023, she graduated with a degree in Historical and Philosophical Theology and Modern Hebrew from Oral Roberts University, earning the honor of Outstanding Theology Student of the Year. Since her graduation, Isabell has become an integral member of the Marilyn & Sarah team in writing, teaching and ministry operations.

Isabell enjoys leading a C.S. Lewis book club at her church, spending time with her friends, reading, dancing, crocheting, traveling, cooking, and watching movies.

For more about Saving Moses,
visit savingmoses.org

For more about Sarah,
visit sarahbowling.org

For more about Marilyn and Sarah Ministries,
visit marilynandsarah.org

endnotes

1   "Trauma," *APA.org*, 2023, https://www.apa.org/topics/trauma.

2   "Who Are You?" Genius.com, July 14, 1978, https://genius.com/The-who-who-are-you-lyrics.

3   "This Flag Flies No More," *Newser.com*, July 10, 2015, https://www.newser.com/story/209631/this-flag-flies-no-more.html.

4   "Black South Carolina Trooper Explains Why He Helped a White Supremacist," *NYTimes.com*, July 25, 2015, https://www.nytimes.com/2015/07/26/us/black-south-carolina-trooper-explains-why-he-embraced-a-white-supremacist.html?hp&action=click&pgtype=Homepage&module=second-column-region®ion=top-news&WT.nav=top-news&_r=0.

5   Arden Dier, "Black Cop's Kindness to White Supremacist Hailed," *Newser.com*, July 20, 2015, https://www.newser.com/story/210084/black-cops-kindness-to-white-supremacist-hailed.html.

6   Rob Quinn, "9 Killed in a Charleston Church Shooting," *Newser.com*, July 17, 2015, https://www.newser.com/story/208493/multiple-fatalities-in-sc-church-shooting.html.

7   Polly Davis Doig, "Black Cop: Why I Helped That White Supremacist," *Newser.com*, July 26, 2015, https://www.newser.com/story/210367/black-cop-why-i-helped-that-white-supremacist.html.

8   Osvaldo Gutierrez, "Veterans Share Their Stories of Experiencing PTSD and How They've Healed," *CV4A.org*, June 24, 2022, https://cv4a.org/the-overwatch/veterans-share-stories-ptsd-healing/.

9   Anne Lora Scagluisi, "4 Women Open Up About What It's Really Like Living with Post-Traumatic Stress Disorder," *Vogue.In*, June 13, 2021, https://www.vogue.in/wellness/content/post-traumatic-stress-disorder-four-women-talk-experience-effects.

10 John P. Rafferty, Kenneth Pletcher, "Japan Earthquake and Tsunami of 2011," *Britannica.com*, August 26, 2023, https://www.britannica.com/event/Japan-earthquake-and-tsunami-of-2011.

11 "Scourge; Scourging," *BibleStudyTools.com*, 2023, https://www.biblestudytools.com/dictionary/scourge-scourging/.

12 "Levite," *Britannica.com*, 2023, https://www.britannica.com/topic/Levite.

13 "The Help," *YouTube.com*, 2011, https://www.youtube.com/watch?v=3H50IlsHm3k from the movie *The Help*, Tate Taylor, Walt Disney Studios Motion Pictures, 2011.